101 Creative Problem Solving Techniques

The Handbook of New Ideas for Business

James M. Higgins

Crummer Graduate School of Business
Rollins College
James M. Higgins & Associates Inc.

THE NEW
MANAGEMENT
PUBLISHING COMPANY
400 North New York Avenue, Suite 215
Winter Park, Florida 32789

DEVELOPMENTAL EDITOR: Carolyn D. Smith

PRODUCTION MANAGER: Susan Novotny

DESIGNER: Keri Caffrey

ILLUSTRATOR: Keri Caffrey

WORD PROCESSOR: Susan Crabill

New Management Publishing Company, Inc.
400 North New York Avenue, Suite 215
Winter Park, Florida 32789

Publisher's Cataloging-in-Publication Data
Higgins, James M.
101 Creative Problem Solving Techniques: The Handbook of New Ideas for Business/James M. Higgins.
p.   cm.
Includes bibliographical references and index.
ISBN 1-883629-00-4
1. Problem solving. @. Organizational change. I. Title. II. Title: One hundred and one creative problem solving techniques.

HD30.29.H54 1994
658.4'063
QBI93-22664

93-8702
P-CIP

Printing   56789

This book is dedicated to my wife Susan, and my mother, Edna, for their loving encouragement of my creativity and innovation.

PREFACE

Businesses and their managers, professional staff, team leaders and other employees are confronted with a host of challenges as they approach the twenty first century. Change is occuring at an accelerating rate. The number of competitors is increasing dramatically. Business is globalizing. New technology is being introduced at a rapid pace. The workforce is increasingly diverse. There is a scarcity of certain resources, including highly skilled workers. There is a transformation occuring from an industrial to a knowledge based society. Economic and market conditions are increasingly unstable, especially on a global basis. Constituents are more demanding. And finally, the entire business environment is becoming more complex.

To meet these challenges and the opportunities they create, businesses are embracing creative problem solving and innovation as never before. To achieve effective and efficient levels of creative problem solving and the innovation which results, an organization must improve the creativity of its work groups and individuals, and it must create the right kind of organizational culture which will turn that creativity into innovation.

One of the key ways in which individuals and groups can improve their creativity is through learning creativity processes, techniques that take advantage of innate intuitive and creative abilities, techniques that channel these abilities to create new or enhanced products or services, or create more effective and efficient organizational processes. This book describes the basic creative problem solving (CPS) model and then describes 101 techniques for unleashing individual and group creativity. These techniques follow the CPS model.

Managers, professionals, team leaders, and any other employee interested in improving his or her job performance or that of the work group, or for that matter, the entire company, will find this book beneficial. This book is readily useable in company training programs. Organizational creativity training programs have grown rapidly in recent months, and this book is designed to meet the needs of such programs.

Two other books by this same author, both to be published in 1995, discuss the other two aspects of increasing organizational innovation. *Innovate or Evaporate: Test and Improve Your Organization's IQ—Its Innovation Quotient,* identifies the set of characteristics common to the innovative organization. It provides numerous descriptions of organizational programs for achieving high levels of innovation performance. *Escape from the Maze: Increasing Personal and Group Creativity* provides a roadmap for improving individual and group creativity performance. For individuals, this means learning to overcome the psychological barriers to creativity imposed by society and the organization, and learning how to increase levels of intuition. For the group, this means learning proper group dynamics to take advantage of group creativity processes. Order forms for the books can be found in the latter pages of this book.

THANKS

No book is the work of the author alone. I want to thank several people for their critical inputs into this book. First, Keri Caffrey, one of the most creative people I've ever known, has illustrated and designed this book in an artful yet fun manner for the reader. Susan Crabill spent several hundred hours working through numerous drafts, all done with great patience. Susan Novotny managed to put all of this together in the final hectic stages of production. Carolyn Smith, my developmental editor on two of my college texts, did an outstanding job of making this book user friendly. Several hundred MBA students provided important feedback about the book, and how to make it more useable. My business reviewers, Phil Harris, Vice President and General Manager of Paperboard for the James River Corporation, Allan Nagle, former CEO of Tupperware, Valerie Oberle, Vice President, Walt Disney Companies, and Rod Waddell, quality consultant and President of Dynamic Resource Development, Inc., have provided important insights about the potential impact of this book. And finally, my wife Susan, has provided tremendous support during this lengthy writing and publication process.

TABLE OF CONTENTS

Chapter 3
CREATIVE TECHNIQUES FOR ANALYZING THE ENVIRONMENT, RECOGNIZING & IDENTIFYING PROBLEMS, AND MAKING ASSUMPTIONS

Chapter 4
INDIVIDUAL TECHNIQUES FOR GENERATING ALTERNATIVES

Chapter 5
GROUP TECHNIQUES FOR
GENERATING ALTERNATIVES

Chapter 6
CREATIVE TECHNIQUES FOR CHOOSING AMONG THE ALTERNATIVES, IMPLEMENTATION, AND CONTROL

Chapter 7
USING THE TECHNIQUES

CHAPTER 1

Creativity &
Innovation
•
The "Four Ps"
•
Four Types of
Innovation

INNOVATE OR EVAPORATE

Profit, thy name is creativity.

— Business Week

When giant PC chipmaker Intel was confronted with new and unusually tough competitors that used clones of its chips to compete on price, CEO Andrew Grove turned to innovation. Intel launched an accelerated schedule for new-product development that produced the 386, 486, and Pentium chips and left competitors in the dust.[1]

When Johnson & Johnson, the health care and consumer products conglomerate, found itself at a cost disadvantage compared to competitors, it launched a program to develop innovative processes that would cut overhead costs. For example, CEO Ralph Larsen created customer support centers, employee teams working on customer sites to facilitate distribution and ordering. The teams eliminated overlapping services in most of the firm's 166 businesses.[2]

When Nordstrom, the Seattle-based department store chain, analyzed its markets, it realized that providing high levels of customer service would be an innovative marketing approach in the discount-oriented retail industry. That strategy worked extremely well, giving Nordstrom an edge in a rapidly changing marketplace.[3]

When Hewlett-Packard realized that it was at a competitive disadvantage in global markets because bureaucratic requirements were slowing the product development process, it redesigned its organizational structure to speed up product development.[4]

Surviving and prospering in business have never been easy. There are always problems to be solved and opportunities to be taken advantage of. But during the next few years, from now through the first decade of the 21st century, business organizations, their managers, and their other employees will be confronted with a number of strategic challenges unmatched in business history. The primary challenges are these:[5]

1. Every facet of business is changing at an accelerating rate.
2. Competition is increasing.
3. Business is becoming increasingly global in scope.
4. New technologies are being introduced at a breathtaking rate.
5. The composition of the work force is changing, as are its members' values and expectations.
6. There are increasing shortages of resources ranging from water to skilled employees.
7. The U.S. economy is being transformed from an industrial economy to one based on knowledge and information.
8. Market and economic conditions throughout the world are extremely unstable.
9. Constituents, such as shareholders and environmentalists, are making greater demands on the organization.
10. Not only is the business environment changing rapidly, but it is becoming much more complex.

As a consequence of these challenges, every facet of business, from overall strategy to daily operations, is full of new problems and opportunities. And the task of just "doing business" remains. This in itself is difficult enough without all of these additional burdens. How can a business or any part of it survive and prosper in the face of such challenges?

By innovating! Virtually every leading authority on business, including Fortune 500 CEOs, researchers, and consultants, agrees that there is only one way firms can cope with all the challenges confronting them in the 1990s, not to mention those they'll have to face in the twenty-first century. They must be innovative.[6] Intel, Johnson & Johnson, Nordstrom, and Hewlett-Packard all innovated in order to survive and prosper. **Innovate or evaporate.**

INNOVATION AND CREATIVITY

Innovation is how a firm or an individual makes money from creativity. Organizations, their managers, and other employees seek to create original ideas and concepts that will end up as innovations, such as new or enhanced products or services, processes that increase efficiency, highly competitive marketing campaigns, or superior management. The process of generating something new is known as **origination**.

Something **original** is something new, something that didn't exist before. **Creativity** is the process of generating something new that has value. There are many original ideas and concepts, but some may not have value and hence may not be considered creative. A **creation** is something original that has value.

Innovation is the process of creating something new that has significant value to an individual, a group, an organization, an industry, or a society. An **innovation** thus is a creation that has significant value.

These distinctions may seem superficial and academic, but they are not. This is so for several reasons, all of which are related to the ultimate goal of innovation. First, you need to learn how to tell whether the ideas you generate are creative or merely original. Original ideas just aren't enough. Second, to be innovative you need to go beyond merely being creative. You need to know whether the ideas you generate have the potential for significant value, that is, the potential to become innovations. Finally, firms as well as individuals must learn to turn creations into innovations. Unfortunately, while U.S. firms and their employees are not nearly as creative as they should be, their performance record is even worse when it comes to turning creations into innovations. On average, only one idea in ten that is developed in a laboratory ever gets to market.[7] As a result, the global competitive positions of U.S. firms have eroded significantly in recent years and will continue to do so unless those firms become more innovative.

Moreover, in meeting the other strategic challenges and in "doing business" every day, firms will not be as effective or efficient as they should be if they cannot be innovative. Solving problems and pursuing opportunities require solutions, many of which may be unique to the specific situation. Therefore, creativity and the resultant innovation are fundamental to the survival and prosperity of the firm.

Creativity, the Springboard to Innovation

Before we can have innovation, we must have creativity.

Expanding on our earlier definition, **creativity**, then, is the skill to originate the new and to make the new valuable.[8] The new key word is **skill**. *Creativity is a skill. It is not something mystical, available only to a few. It can be learned by anyone. Everyone possesses an innate capacity for creativity. But the development of this capacity into a skill has been thwarted, for the most part by parents, teachers, and bosses who provide and enforce rules about what is acceptable behavior and because only a few* *behaviors are allowed, creativity is stifled. Therefore, you must act to develop this skill, to unleash your untapped potential. This book is about becoming more creative by learning techniques which enhance creativity in problem solving.*

Creativity can be incremental, occurring in a series of small progressive steps, such as the lengthy, painstaking research that led to the development of polio vaccine. Conversely, creativity can involve giant leaps of progress in which many links in the evolutionary chain of concepts are hurdled by a single effort. The main workings of Apple Computer's MacIntosh personal computer, a highly advanced system, were a giant leap in technology at the time that they were introduced.

The product of the creative effort need not be a tangible physical object. It may be an idea, an association of facts, an insight, or a more effective or efficient process as well as a new product or service. Each of these, when fully expressed and functioning, has value.

For an organization, one of the critical steps in achieving innovation is developing the creative problem-solving skills of its human resources—its managers, professionals, and other employees. This book is designed to help in developing those skills. The following chapters present **101** techniques or processes for making problem solving more creative.

THE "FOUR P'S" OF CREATIVITY AND INNOVATION

Important to raising levels of creativity and innovation is an understanding of the **"four P's:" product**, **possibilities**, **processes** (techniques), and **personal and group** creativity. The first of the **four P's,** the product or result, will not occur unless the other **three P's** are in place. (See Figure 1.1)

If a firm, group, or organization is not moving to further its innovation—that is, if it is not providing the correct **possibilities** (the right organizational culture) or educating its members in the right individual or group creative **processes**, or developing its members' levels of **personal and group** creativity—it will not be able to cope with the ten strategic challenges identified earlier, nor will it be able to solve its other problems as well as it might otherwise. It won't have the **products** it needs to survive and prosper.

How the 4 P'S Fit Together with Creativity and Innovation

Creativity can be increased both by learning techniques (processes) and by increasing personal and group creativity. If these occur within the right organizational culture (possibilities), the result is innovation, as shown in Figure 1.1.

Figure 1.1 How the Four Ps Relate to Each Other

Creativity	+	Organizational Culture	=	Innovation
Processes (Techniques) Personal and Group Creativity		Possibilities		Product 4 Types of Innovation: Product, Process, Marketing, Management

The Product

The **product** is the result of the creation/innovation process. It can be a physical product, a service, or an enhancement to these; a process for increasing effectiveness and/or efficiency; a more innovative approach to marketing, or a better way to manage. To be a true creative product it must have value and not just be original. To be innovative, it must have significant value.

How do you determine what has potentially significant value? Sometimes by analysis. Sometimes by intuition. Value is relative, both to the value systems of the evaluator and to the time during which the creation occurs. For example, twelve Hollywood studios turned down the "Star Wars" movie concept. Finally Twentieth Century Fox agreed to take the risk and made the most financially successful movie of all time. Similarly, some inventors and their investors offered to sell a new idea to IBM, General Motors, DuPont, and several other major firms and were turned down by all of them. Finally, they decided to build and market the product themselves and became multimillionaires. The process was photocopying. The company became Xerox.[9]

Even successful entrepreneurs may misjudge the value of a creation and, hence, its potential to become an innovation. Victor Kiam, of Remington Razor fame, was once offered the patent to Velcro for $25,000; he turned it down, believing it had no future.[10] Velcro products have sold for about $6 billion since their inception through 1988.

Later in this book, in Chapter 6, some ways for determining whether a product is innovative will be discussed.

The Possibilities

For innovation to occur, the **possibilities** for creativity and innovation must exist. Regardless of your creative talents, however great your knowledge or skill, you will not be able to create many innovations if you are not functioning in a favorable situation. If the organization's culture, in the broadest sense, does not support and even require innovation, it is unlikely that innovation will occur. The evidence indicates that organizational innovation results from careful management of the organization's culture. This can be readily understood in terms of managing the "**seven S's**" of organizational success:[11] strategy, structure, systems (management), style (leadership), staffing, skills (sought synergies), and shared values (organizational culture). The term <u>shared values</u> includes values related to the other six **S's**.

The Processes

Numerous techniques can be used to increase the creativity of problem solving within an organization. Learning these takes time and effort but you can master them. These processes are directed at increasing creativity in all stages of the problem-solving process. Chapters 3, 4, 5, and 6 review these techniques for individuals and groups.

Personal and Group Creativity

Increasing **personal creativity** involves a two-pronged effort: increasing the use of the right brain (left brain if left handed) to raise your levels of intuition, and freeing yourself from socialization that has restricted your creativity. The latter includes not only resocializing yourself but also learning new habits that will help you be more creative. The individual functions within a group, so it is very important to properly manage **group** dynamics in order to increase **creativity.**

A Trilogy of Books on Creativity and Innovation

These four P's are the subjects of the three books in this series, which form a trilogy on creativity and innovation.

1. *101 Creative Problem Solving Techniques: The Handbook of New Ideas for Business* reviews the **processes (techniques)** that individuals and groups can use in the creative problem solving process to make their use of it more creative.

2. *Innovate or Evaporate: Test and Improve Your Organization's IQ—Its Innovation Quotient* discusses both the **product** (the four types of innovation, which are defined briefly in the next section of this chapter) and the **possibilities** for achieving the product.

3. *Escape From the Maze: Increasing Personal and Group Creativity Potential* discusses how to raise **personal creativity** levels by working to improve intuition and by removing barriers to creativity. A brief discussion of how to improve group dynamics in order to improve **group creativity** is included.

THE FOUR TYPES OF INNOVATION

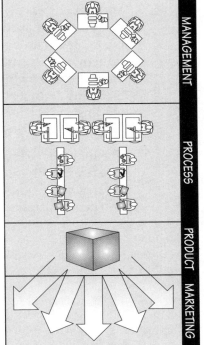

There are four principal types of innovation (the product or result of the innovation effort): product, process, marketing, and management.[12]

1. **Product innovation** results in new products or services, or enhancements to old products or services. The opening paragraph in this chapter on Intel described a product innovation situation.

2. **Process innovation** results in improved processes within the organization—for example, in operations, human resources management, or finance. It focuses on improving effectiveness and efficiency. The Johnson & Johnson example at the beginning of the chapter described process innovation.

3. **Marketing innovation** is related to the marketing functions of promotion, pricing, and distribution, as well as to product functions other than product development (for example, packaging or advertising). Nordstroms, as described in the third paragraph of this chapter, used service as a marketing innovation.

4. **Management innovation** improves the way the organization is managed. Hewlett-Packard's restructuring as discussed in the fourth paragraph of this chapter, was a management innovation.

Studies of successful organizations suggest that they design more new products and concepts, utilize their resources more effectively and efficiently, market their products more creatively, and manage more effectively than less successful organizations.[13]

It is creativity in managing all of the economic functions—marketing, operations, finance, human resources, research and development, and information management that separates the truly successful companies from the less successful ones. This can be seen in the discussion of Steelcase contained in The Innovative Edge in Action 1.1. Note that Steelcase is not a high-tech firm but operates in a basic manufacturing industry. An important lesson to learn from this reading is that innovation is applicable to most jobs in all kinds of industries.

The Innovative Edge in Action 1.2 describes Banc One, a service firm that has found that innovation is necessary for survival. One lesson to learn from this reading is how innovation can be applied in a service industry.

IMPROVING INNOVATION AT STEELCASE

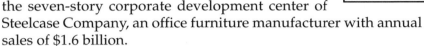

The pyramids of Egypt symbolize a culture that was inert and set in its ways long before its eventual demise. In Grand Rapids, Michigan, there is a pyramid that symbolizes innovation and change. It is the seven-story corporate development center of Steelcase Company, an office furniture manufacturer with annual sales of $1.6 billion.

Like many large, long-established American corporations, Steelcase was making a stodgy and boring, though in this case, high-quality, product. Its closest competitor, Herman Miller, Inc., posed a significant competitive threat because of its innovative spirit. Miller is credited with creating the "open office" by using "systems furniture" based on movable panels and furniture modules, and with leading in the design of the "ergonomic" chair, which constantly adjusts to changes in the user's position. In the 1970s, Steelcase was just a follower.

Seeking to increase its dominance of the market, Steelcase has acquired a number of small, high-profile design companies. It now has a line of wooden office furniture and the rights to furniture designed by architects Frank Lloyd Wright and Le Corbusier. It has also rebuilt its physical facilities and reorganized its operations. The $111 million, 128-foot-tall pyramidal office building, the most visible change, clearly demonstrates the company's new commitment to innovation and style as well as quality.

Previously, the company's designers, engineers, and marketing personnel were housed in separate buildings. Now they are grouped together to facilitate employee interaction, a necessary requirement

CONTINUES ON PAGE 12

THE INNOVATIVE EDGE IN ACTION 1.1

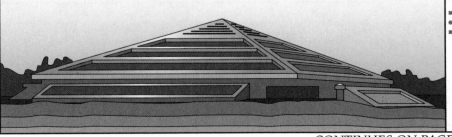

STEELCASE
Continued from page 11

if new and creative products are to be developed (management innovation). However, physical closeness alone does not generate cooperation and innovation. The showpiece building is more than just a flashy shape. Steelcase's idea is that everything that happens there is work, from coffee breaks to board meetings. Every inch of the building is dominated by a light and airy central atrium, called the town square. There are exterior terraces where people can work or eat. Coffee-break stations have marker boards to promote open exchange of ideas, and there are "caves" where individuals can go for solitude.

The new building is already inspiring its employees. The company has introduced a sleek new line of furniture, the Context line (product innovation). In the words of James C. Soule, vice-president of the international division, "The bottom line for us is whether we produce better products." Steelcase is improving its already high quality and cutting costs by adopting autonomous work teams, investing heavily in plant and equipment, and performing work re-engineering (process innovation). A 71-foot pendulum, computerized to follow the sun, has been installed as a symbol of the company's commitment to continuing change. A video about the firm touts its new innovative spirit (marketing innovation).

Sources: Jana Schilder, "Work Teams Boost Productivity," *Personnel Journal* (February 1992), pp. 67–71; Michael A. Verespej, "America's Best Plants: Steelcase," *Industry Week* (October 21, 1992), pp. 53–54; John A. Sheridan, "Frank Merlotti: A Master of Empowerment," *Industry Week* (January 7, 1991), pp. 24–27; Allen E. Alter, "The Corporate Make-Over," *CIO* (December 1990), pp. 32–42; John A. Sheridan, "World-Class Manufacturing (Part 1)," *Industry Week* (July 2, 1990), pp. 36–46; and Gregory Witcher, "Steelcase Hopes Innovation Flourishes Under Pyramid," *Wall Street Journal* (May 26, 1989), pp. B1, B8.

BANC ONE: USING CREATIVITY TO PROSPER

The banking industry has undergone a massive amount of change. Indeed, it is no longer really just the banking industry but the financial services industry. Commercial banks, savings banks, and credit unions now offer services in brokerage, insurance, and financial planning. And because of the trend toward diversification, a "commercial bank" offering a full line of services, such as Banc One, finds itself in competition with domestic rivals such as Sears, American Express, and Merrill Lynch, as well as with global banks and insurance firms. Banks now have to think of themselves as retailers. They have to create visual excitement, and sell to their customers when they come into the bank. Competition is increasing and the rate of change in the industry is accelerating.

Banc One's operation in upper Arlington, Ohio looks a lot more like a small shopping mall than it does a bank these days. It incorporates several small boutiques, an insurance agency, a real estate office, a travel agency, and a discount stock brokerage (product innovations). Across from these boutiques, at the bank itself, are three tellers, an automated teller machine, and a new-accounts desk. The impact of a high-tech decor is heightened by large, bright informational banners (marketing innovations). "This is a survival issue," says John F. Fisher, senior vice president of Banc One Corporation, Banc One's parent company. "Our old branches don't work for what we need them for today, we must learn to compete with Sears and K-Mart [which offers banking at some stores] in all the things they do."

Banc One uses several techniques to maintain its creative edge. It works hard to develop new products. For example, in 1993, 400 branches opened personal investment centers where customers can receive investment counseling (product innovation). But, it innovates not only in products but in processes, marketing, and management as well. One of its principal strategies for success is bringing its unique version of tight controls to the banks it acquires. Yet, unlike other acquisition oriented banks, it doesn't fire

THE INNOVATIVE EDGE IN ACTION 1.2

CONTINUES ON PAGE 14

13

BANC ONE

Continued from page 13

the staffs of the banks it acquires, rather it works closely with them to show them how the other banks in a group became successful, and it cajoles them into following suit (management innovation). In a different area of control. It has even developed a video which it sends to delinquent credit card accounts. This video has resulted in increased payments and reduced delinquency rates (process innovation). It is considered to have leading edge technological applications in several areas (process innovation). Finally, it has produced a series of clever ads touting its resources (marketing innovation).

Many bankers are not prepared for such changes. They cannot utilize their computers fully and are not prepared to make creative decisions, having spent much of their careers in a regulated environment with almost guaranteed returns on investment. With limited competition and no change, decision making was routine and programmed. Largely structured, easy decision rules were available. That is not the case any more.

The bank that intends to survive has to be creative and competitive. Research has shown that a creative individual makes better decisions than one who is strictly rational. This is as true of bankers as of anyone else.

Source: "Banc One Corporation 1992 Annual Report," (Columbus, Ohio: Banc One, February 1993), pp. 5–10; "Banc One: Mightier Than Its Parts," *Economist* (December 19, 1992), p. 76; James S. Hirsch, "Growing Ambition: Fast-Rising Banc One, Already Big in Texas, Looks at Other Areas," *Wall Street Journal*, December 26, 1990, pp. A2, A10; Steve Weiner, "Banks Hire Retailing Consultants for Helping Become Financial Products Stores," *Wall Street Journal*, May 20, 1986, p. 31.

REFERENCES

1 Robert D. Hof, "Inside Intel: It's Moving Double-Time to Head Off Competitors," *Business Week* (June 1, 1992), pp. 86–94.

2 Joseph Weber, "A Big Company That Works," *Business Week* (May 4, 1992), pp. 124–132.

3 Barry Farber and Joyce Wycoff, "Customer Service: Evolution and Revolution," *Sales & Marketing Management* (May 1991), pp. 44–51; Susan Caminiti, "The New Champions of Retailing," *Fortune* (September 24, 1990), pp. 85–100; Dori Jones Yang and Laura Zinn, "Will 'The Nordstrom Way' Travel Well?" *Business Week* (September 3, 1990), pp. 82–83.

4 Stephen Kreider Yoder, "Quick Change: A 1990 Reorganization at Hewlett-Packard Already is Paying Off," *Wall Street Journal* (July 22, 1991), pp. A1, A8; Barbara Buell and Robert D. Hof, "Hewlett-Packard Rethinks Itself," *Business Week* (April 1, 1991), pp. 76–78.

5 James M. Higgins, *The Management Challenge: An Introduction to Management 2nd ed.* (New York: Macmillan, 1994) Chapter 1; James M. Higgins and Julian W. Vincze, *Strategic Management: Text and Cases, 5th ed.*, (Dallas: Dryden Press, 1993) Chapter 1.

6 For example see: William P. Hewlett (chairman and co-founder of Hewlett-Packard), "Graduation Speech" as reported in Helen Pike, "Hewlett Sounds Call for Engineering Creativity in MIT Graduate Speech," *Electronic Engineering Times* (June 23, 1986), p. 78; John Sculley (then CEO and chairman of Apple Computer), "Speech to MacWorld," February 1988 in which he indicated that only the innovative firm would survive in the future; Jack Welch (CEO and chairman of General Electric), who sees innovation driving productivity which drives competition, as quoted in Thomas A. Stewart, "GE Keeps Those Ideas Coming," *Fortune* (August 12, 1991), pp. 41–49; Michael E. Porter (researcher and consultant), *The Competitive Advantage of Nations* (New York: Free Press, 1990) pp. 578–579 where he observes that innovation, continuous improvement and change are the cornerstones of global competitiveness; Michael E. Porter; *Competitive Strategy* (New York: Free Press, 1980) pp. 177–179 where he discusses the criticality of innovation to competitiveness; a 1987 survey of 1000 CEOs by consulting firm Arthur D. Little found that 92 percent believed that innovation was critical to the future success of their firm — "Common Sense, Experiences Are Not Enough: It's Time to Get Creative," *Marketing News* (January 18, 1988), p. 7; Richard N. Foster (consultant), *Innovation: The Attacker's Advantage* (New York: Summitt Books, 1986) p. 21 where he indicates that in his thirty years at McKinsey & Company, every successful firm he saw was innovative; Thomas J. Peters (consultant and researcher), *Thriving on Chaos: Handbook for a Management Revolution* (New York: Knopf, 1987) pp. 191–280 where he indicates that innovation is one of five prescriptions for chaos (accelerating change, complex environment, global competition, and other challenges); *Business Week* considered the topic of innovation so critical to U.S. competitiveness, it devoted two special issues to it, in June in both 1989 and 1990.

7 Amal Kumar Naj, "Creative Energy: GE's Latest Invention—A Way to Move Ideas From Lab to Market," *Wall Street Journal* (June 14, 1990), pp. A1, A9.

8 John G. Young, "What is Creativity?" *The Journal of Creative Behavior* (1985, 2nd Quarter), pp. 77-87.

9 "Chester Carlson—Xerography," Xerox Internal Documents; "A Profile in Entrepreneurship," a special advertising session, *Inc.* (July 1988), pp. 109, 110.

10 Victor Kiam, speech to the Roy E. Crummer Graduate School of Business, Rollins College, Winter Park, FL (October 28, 1985).

11 Thomas J. Peters and Robert H. Waterman, Jr., *In Search of Excellence*, (New York: Harper & Row, 1982) pp. 9–11. Adapted slightly from their seven Ss model—strategy, structure, systems, style, staff, skills, shared values (culture).

12 Ray Statta, "Organizational Learning — The Key to Management Innovation," *Sloan Management Review* (Spring 1989), pp. 63-74; Michael Porter, *Competitive Strategy*, (New York: Free Press, 1980) pp. 177-178.

13 For example see, Richard Foster, loc. cit.; Thomas J. Peters, loc. cit.

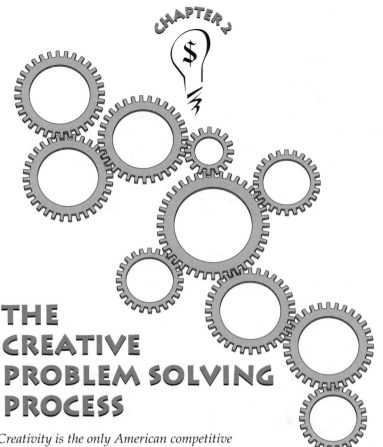

Creative
Problem
Solving Stages
•
Building
Creativity Into
Problem
Solving
•
101
CPS
Techniques

THE CREATIVE PROBLEM SOLVING PROCESS

Creativity is the only American competitive advantage left.

— John G. Young
Former CEO, Hewlett-Packard

Problem solving is an integral part of organizational life. Everytime a manager or leader directs people in producing a product or service, problems are being solved, decisions made. Every time any member of an organization thinks of a new way to reduce costs, invents a new product or service, or determines how to help the organization function better in some way, problem solving is taking place. But, whether the problem solving occurring in these situations is truly creative is another question, one that deserves a closer look.

For individuals, the development of creative problem-solving skills is a necessity, not a luxury. Because organizations too must solve problems, the development of these skills in their members is also a necessity. The most innovative individuals and organizations are the ones most likely to survive and prosper.

This chapter will show you how to start solving problems more creatively or more creatively taking advantage of opportunities, both on the job and elsewhere. The chapter begins by describing the traditional problem-solving process as practiced by business people for many years. It then discusses how problem solving can be made more creative. It thus sets the stage for examining the aspects of problem solving in which creativity may be used to its fullest extent.

CREATIVE PROBLEM SOLVING

Not too many years ago, problem solving was defined largely as a rational effort.[1] As scientists and management researchers tried to improve the problem-solving process, they focused on analysis and quantitative factors. But in recent years we have come to realize that a strictly rational approach misses the whole point of problem solving. Creativity is vital to successful problem solving. The problem-solving pro-

Figure 2.1 The Creative Problem-Solving (CPS) Process

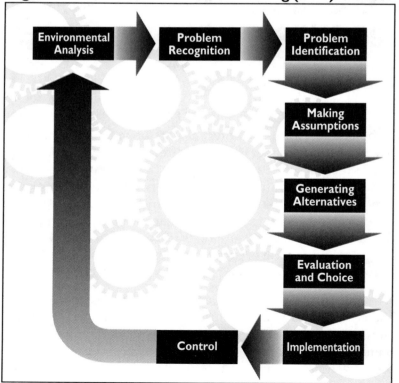

cess therefore has come to be referred to as the creative problem-solving process or CPS.

There are eight basic stages in the **creative problem solving process:** analyzing the environment, recognizing a problem, identifying the problem, making assumptions, generating alternatives, choosing among alternatives, implementing the chosen solution, and control.

Figure 2.2 Four Stages of the CPS Process

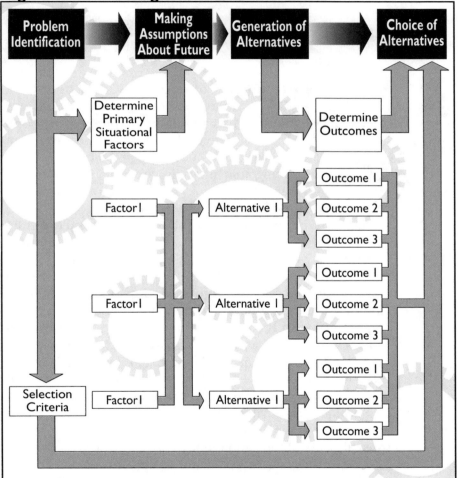

These stages are shown in Figure 2.1. The middle four of these stages are shown in the more detailed diagram presented in Figure 2.2. This figure provides more detail on these four stages primarily to show how the decision maker goes from problem identification and the selection of criteria to the actual choice of a decision. The following paragraphs briefly examine these stages from the practical viewpoint of problem solving within an organization. Personal, non-work-related problem solving would follow the same stages. Both analytical and creative processes are applicable to all eight stages.

Analyzing the Environment

If you're not constantly searching for problems (which, as defined here, include opportunities), how will you know if they exist? And how can you solve problems or take advantage of opportunities if you don't know they exist? Most strategists believe that firms must be prepared to respond quickly to problems and opportunities in order to be successful in the future.[2] Thus, being able to recognize problems and opportunities as soon as they occur, or even before they occur, is vital to success. Both internal and external organizational environments must be constantly and carefully monitored for signs of problems or opportunities. In this stage of the process, you are gathering information. Information gained during the control stage of CPS is vital to this stage of the process. See Figure 2.1. Royal Dutch Shell Oil Company spends millions of dollars annually tracking its competition and the economy, and learning about its customers, for just one type of information system—the strategic information system. It also trains all levels of management to look for weak signals of environmental change. It spends thousands of man-hours creating forecasts/scenarios of possible futures, all to enable it to solve strategic and operational problems better.[3] The individual problem solver must also spend time and money searching the environment looking for signals of problems or opportunities. For example, spend a few minutes to look at your internal and external organization environments. What is happening that might lead to problems or opportunities?

Recognizing a Problem

You need to be aware that a problem or opportunity exists before you can solve it or take advantage of it. It is from the information gathered in analyzing the environment that you will learn that a problem or opportunity exists. Often, however, the problem solver has only a vague feeling that something is wrong or that an opportunity exists. A gestation period seems to occur in which information from the environment is processed subconsciously and the existence of a problem or opportunity eventually registers at the conscious level.[4] For example, when Mikio Kitano, Toyota's production guru, began analyzing the firm's manufacturing cost information in the early 1990s, he intuitively sensed that something was wrong. The firm simply wasn't saving as much money as it should from all of the automation and robotization that it had just completed. He believed it was because robots were being used when human beings could do the job just as well, at less cost. Other top managers doubted him, but in the end he proved that he was right saving Toyota millions of dollars in unnecessary investment.[5]

Identifying the Problem

The problem identification stage involves making sure the organization's efforts will be directed toward solving the real problem rather than merely eliminating symptoms.[6] This stage also involves establishing the objectives of the problem-solving process and determining what will constitute evidence that the problem has been solved. The outcome of this stage is a set of decision criteria for evaluating various options. See Figure 2.2.

Both rational and intuitive thinking may occur at this stage, but identification is largely a rational process. Key questions to be asked include the following:[7]

1. What happened or will happen?

2. Who does it or will it affect?

3. Where did it or will it have an impact?

4. When did it or will it happen?

5. How did it or will it occur?

6. Why did it or will it occur?

7. What could we do to be more successful?

In asking these questions you are primarily interested in getting to the core problem or identifying the real opportunity. The benefits of doing so are aptly illustrated by the case of Frito-Lay, described in The Innovative Edge in Action 2.1.

Making Assumptions

It is necessary to make assumptions about the condition of future factors in the problem situation. For example, what will the state of the economy be when the new product is to be launched? Or, how will your manager react to a suggestion? Remember that assumptions may be a major constraint on the potential success of a solution, or may cause you to overestimate the potential of a particular alternative to solve the problem effectively. One of my assumptions in writing this book was that there was a growing number of people interested in innovation processes. Therefore, this book would sell many copies. When I started in 1985, my assumption was wrong. But by 1993 it was right.

AT FRITO-LAY, CPS IS A KEY TO SUCCESS

Frito-Lay, the $3.5 billion a year in sales, Dallas-based snack food company first initiated a CPS program in 1983. From 1983 to 1987, the firm documented cost savings and improved productivity of $500 million directly attributable to CPS. Profits grew at a compounded rate of 12.7% annually, twice as fast as sales. Similar successes were believed to exist in product development, but figures were not tracked. Introduced in 1983, CPS at Frito-Lay occurs in eight steps: (1) finding the problem, (2) collecting the facts, (3) defining the problem, (4) generating ideas for its solution, (5) evaluating and selecting the best ideas, (6) creating a plan of action, (7) selling the idea to senior management, and (8) putting the solution into action. According to group manager of product supply, Louis Kosmin, the heart of CPS is not finding a solution but finding the real problem.

With CPS training, a person learns methods for anticipating problems, identifying problems, generating alternatives, and initiating new projects. A major part of CPS at Frito-Lay involves training employees in many of the processes discussed in this book. The company views the generation of alternatives as a critical part of CPS. Frito-Lay has taught CPS to some of its major vendors and introduced it to its sister companies, Pizza Hut and Kentucky Fried Chicken. Frito-Lay procurement has conducted introductory CPS workshops for sixteen major suppliers.

Historically, CPS at Frito-Lay focused on improving operations. Only late in its life span was it used for new product R&D. Sunchips, Frito-Lay's extremely successful snack food, was one product which resulted from CPS. In 1991, new management at Frito-Lay surprisingly abandoned a formal CPS program.

Frank Prince, formerly the director of CPS for Frito-Lay, offered this example of how CPS worked at Frito-Lay. Members of the planning group from Florida, Georgia, and North and South Carolina were meeting to discuss how to improve business in their areas. These groups consisted of plant managers, logistics managers, and sales managers from plants or territories in these four

CONTINUES ON PAGE 24

23

THE INNOVATIVE EDGE IN ACTION 2.1

FRITO-LAY
Continued from page 23

states. Breakage became a hot issue at one point. Typically, each manager had defended his own turf on the issue. Plant managers blamed logistics for breakage, logistics blamed the plant for poor quality containers and packaging. Sales, which included retail unit servicers, was blamed by both for the rough treatment of items at point of display. By working together and by using CPS, this cross functional group discovered ways they could help solve this problem. For example, they made changes in the way that products were stacked in the delivery trucks, and in the way products were stacked within containers. Both solutions were successful.

Source: Telephone discussion with Frank Prince, partner, Involvement Systems, Dallas, Texas, September 1993; Marc Hequet, "Making Creativity Training Creative," *Training* February 1992, p. 45; Cathy Handley, "Why Frito-Lay Is Crackling with New Ideas," *Purchasing*, May 3, 1990, pp. 84A2-84A5.

Generating Alternatives

Generating alternatives involves cataloging the known options (a rational act) and generating additional options (a rational and intuitive act). *It is in this stage that most of the creativity processes described in later chapters are very helpful.*

To the extent that you can clearly identify and formulate useful options, you can maximize the chances that a problem will be solved satisfactorily. The purpose of generating alternatives is to ensure that you reach the selection stage of CPS with enough potential solutions. Creative techniques for generating alternatives can help you develop many more possible solutions than you might come up with otherwise.

Generating alternatives is partly a rational and partly an intuitive exercise. It's rational in that you follow a series of steps. It's intuitive in that these steps are designed to unleash your intuitive powers so that you can use them effectively. In this stage, you should be more interested in the quantity of new ideas than in their quality. For most people, creativity reaches its highest levels in this stage of CPS. When Apple Computer Corporation's engineers designed the "Newton," the firm's new personal digital assistant computer (a small computer designed to help people in a wide range of jobs), they generated hundreds of alternative capabilities for the machine. In the end, several major ones were chosen over the others.[8] The Innovative Edge in Action 2.2 describes the less glamorous task of process innovation at Eaton Corporation, and the way that alternatives are generated.

Choosing Among Alternatives

Decision making should be based on a systematic evaluation of the alternatives against the criteria established earlier. A key, very rational part of this process involves determining the possible outcomes of the various alternatives. (See Figure 2.2) This information is vital in making a decision. The better the job done in generating alternatives and determining their possible outcomes, the greater the chance that an effective choice will be made. The choice process is mostly rational, but very skilled decision makers rely on intuition as well, especially for complex problems.

When Honda engineers pioneered the development of an engine that would get 55 miles per gallon, they had several alternatives to choose from. Important to their decision of the technology they chose, were the impacts of the new technology on the costs of production, compatibility with existing transmissions, and so on. Each possible technology had to be evaluated for its impact on these factors.[9] Similarly, McDonalds Corporation, in considering new menu items for its fast food restaurants, has hundreds to choose from. Each potential menu item has to be evaluated against important criteria such as freezability (all McDonalds' ready-made foods are frozen), compatability with other menu items, taste, customer demand, and cost/price relationships. They chose items like pizza because it fit these criteria.[10] Conversely when Wayne Sanders, head of

Kimberly-Clark's diaper division bet on Huggies Pull-Ups, he did so totally from intuition. The product looked promising but development proved difficult. He stayed with the product and eventually he was proven right. At the end of 1991, the product had 31% of the U.S. market.[11]

Implementation

Once you have a clear idea of what you want to do and a plan for accomplishing it, you can take action. Implementation requires persistent attention. This means accounting for details and anticipating and overcoming obstacles. Set specific goals and reasonable deadlines, and gain the support of others for your solution. Implementation is a series of problems and opportunities. The processes described in this book are applicable to each of these.

When General Mills Restaurants, a subsidiary of General Mills, Inc., began a total quality management program for its Olive Garden chain, it paved the way for adaptation at all sites by providing a lengthy training and development program. In addition, success stories were chronicled and distributed on video tape to all restaurants.[12]

Control

Evaluating results is the final, and often overlooked, stage in the creative problem-solving process. The purpose of the evaluation is to determine the extent to which the actions you took have solved the problem. This stage feeds directly into the environmental analysis stage, which begins a new cycle of creative problem solving. It is important at this stage to be able to recognize deficiencies in your own solutions if necessary. If you can admit to making mistakes or changing your mind without feeling defensive or embarrassed, you have acquired the skill of open minded

EATON CORPORATION USES PROCESS INNOVATION TO COMPETE

Eaton Corporation manufactures gears, engine valves, truck axles, circuit breakers, and other unglamorous parts, largely for automobile manufacturers. It has 38,000 employees in 110 plants around the world. It prospers through obsessive cost cutting and other actions to increase productivity. Some of the actions it takes are classic in nature, for example, closing less productive plants and shifting work from union plants in the northern U.S. to nonunion plants in the southern U.S. and Mexico. But the main program which has enabled it to make its U.S. plants more productive is its version of continuous improvement.

Employees routinely make decisions about how to improve productivity throughout Eaton Corporation plants. They have bought into productivity improvement efforts, and have been empowered through teams to make the decisions necessary to enable the firm to become more productive. Eaton has opened its books to employees to help them make more informed decisions. And through plant wide gainsharing programs, recognition awards, and other reward programs, Eaton has motivated employees to actively seek process innovations. *Esprit de corps* is high. Teams with names like ferrets and worms meet regularly to solve problems. Many alternatives are generated before final solutions are implemented.

Examples of process innovation abound. For example, by making numerous small changes in production activities, one group of workers was able to cut scrap by 50 percent. And while solving the scrap cutting problem, these same workers learned to preheat dies before using them, saving the company $50,000 a year in one plant alone. Employees built two automated machines on the shop floor for $80,000 and $93,000 rather than buy them from vendors for $350,000 and $250,000 respectively. And workers have designed effective compensation programs that raise compensation as workers progress through stages of job knowledge rather than insisting that the company pay workers full wages to new hires before they are fully productive as would have normally happened in a union contract situation.

Source: Thomas F. O'Boyle, "Working Together: A Manufacturer Grows Efficient by Soliciting Ideas from Employees," *Wall Street Journal*, June 5, 1992, pp. A1, A4.

THE INNOVATIVE EDGE IN ACTION 2.2

adaptation. This often requires objective thinking, intellectual courage, and self-confidence. At Federal Express, group decisions based on CPS are part of the everyday routine, and so is control. For example when one team solved problems related to sorting packages, they were required to track results and make further improvements.[13]

BUILDING CREATIVITY INTO PROBLEM SOLVING

Experience with problem solving has produced some discouraging findings. Among them are the following:

1. Creativity is not a major part of the problem-solving process for most organizations or individuals.

2. People are not usually encouraged to be creative, either as individuals or as members of organizations. This means that creativity is discouraged in most organizations including families, schools and companies.

3. Few people really know the creative techniques that can be applied in the problem-solving process.

4. Few individuals develop their personal creative problem-solving skills, but that is changing.

It is evident that most people, as well as most organizations, can improve their CPS skills. Typical of the problem are the results of a competition held by General Foods for MBA students from six of the nation's best graduate business schools—Harvard, Chicago, Stanford, Northwestern, Michigan, and Columbia. The task was to come up with solutions to this problem: "Develop a marketing plan to stem the plunging sales of sugar-free Koolaid." The results were disappointing.

The students had an entire day to develop their strategies. Each team was allotted twenty minutes to present its solutions. Judges from General Foods, its advertising agency, and one of its consulting firms evaluated these presentations over a five-hour period. The criteria used were: understanding of the business situation, feasibility and creativity of solutions, and quality of presentation. The students did well in all of these areas except creativity. The judges eventually named Michigan the winner on the strength of its strategic thinking.

Douglas Smith, marketing manager for beverages at General Foods, comments, "There were a couple of ideas that were of interest but nothing we haven't looked at before." Smith continues, "Business schools deal with the left side of the brain, with analysis and facts, but they don't help people much to use the other side, which is judging and intuitive."[14]

101 CPS TECHNIQUES

There are any number of ways to improve creative problem-solving. You might, for example, learn how to improve your intuitive abilities, or you might focus on changing the organization's culture to make it more receptive to creativity. Those are the subjects of other books. The remaining chapters of this book will describe **101** creative techniques that, when used at the appropriate stage of CPS, can greatly improve the results of that process. Techniques are described for environmental analysis, recognizing and identifying problems, making assumptions, generating alternatives, making choices, and implementing solutions. **70** of the **101** techniques described are used to generate alternatives. The following table lists each of the 101 techniques by problem solving stage. Techniques are presented in alphabetical order both in the table and in the chapters. Techniques are numbered twice. The first number denotes the technique's position from 1 to 101, the second number is the technique's position within that section of the problem solving model.

TABLE 2.1 Creativity Techniques by Problem Solving Stage

ENVIRONMENTAL ANALYSIS (Discussed in Chapter 3)

1/1.	Comparisons against others: benchmarking, best practices, racing against phantom competitors
2/2.	Hire futurists, consultants
3/3.	Monitor weak signals
4/4.	Opportunity searches

TABLE CONTINUES ON PAGE 30

TABLE 2.1 Creativity Techniques by Problem Solving Stage

PROBLEM RECOGNITION (Discussed in Chapter 3)

5/1.	Camelot
6/2.	Checklists
7/3.	Inverse brainstorming
8/4.	Limericks and parodies
9/5.	Listing complaints
10/6.	Responding to someone else
11/7.	Role playing
12/8.	Suggestion programs
13/9.	Workouts and other group approaches

PROBLEM IDENTIFICATION (Discussed in Chapter 3)

14/1.	Bounce it off someone else
15/2.	Consensus building
16/3.	Draw a picture of the problem
17/4.	Experience kit
18/5.	Fishbone diagram
19/6.	King of the mountain
20/7.	Redefining the problem or opportunity
21/8.	Rewrite objectives in different ways
22/9.	Squeeze and stretch
23/10.	What do you know?
24/11.	What patterns exist?
25/12.	Why-why diagram

MAKING ASSUMPTIONS (Discussed in Chapter 3)

26/1.	Assumption reversal

GENERATING ALTERNATIVES (Discussed in Chapters 4 and 5)

Individual Techniques (Discussed in Chapter 4)

27/1.	Analogies and metaphors
28/2.	Analysis of past solutions
29/3.	Association
30/4.	Attribute association chains
31/5.	Attribute listing
32/6.	Back to the customer
33/7.	Back to the sun
34/8.	Circle of opportunity
35/9.	Computer programs

TABLE 2.1 Creativity Techniques by Problem Solving Stage

36/10.	Deadlines
37/11.	Direct analogies
38/12.	Establish idea sources
39/13.	Examine it with the senses
40/14.	FCB grid
41/15.	Focused-object technique
42/16.	Fresh eye
43/17.	Idea bits and racking
44/18.	Idea notebook
45/19.	Input-output
46/20.	Listening to music
47/21.	Mind mapping
48/22.	Name possible uses
49/23.	Napoleon technique
50/24.	Organized random search
51/25.	Personal analogies
52/26.	Picture stimulation
53/27.	Product improvement checklist
54/28.	Relatedness
55/29.	Relational words
56/30.	Reversal-dereversal
57/31.	Rolling in the grass of ideas
58/32.	7 X 7 technique
59/33.	Sleeping/dreaming on it
60/34.	Two-words technique
61/35.	Using the computer to stimulate creativity
62/36.	Verbal checklist for creativity
63/37.	Visualization
64/38.	What if ...?

Group Techniques (Discussed in Chapter 5)

65/1.	Brainstorming
66/2.	Brainwriting
67/3.	Brainwriting pool
68/4.	Brainwriting 6-3-5
69/5.	Creative imaging
70/6.	Creative leaps
71/7.	Creativity circles
72/8.	Crawford slip method
73/9.	Delphi technique
74/10.	Excursion technique

TABLE CONTINUES ON PAGE 32

TABLE 2.1 Creativity Techniques by Problem Solving Stage

75/11. Gallery method
76/12. Gordon/Little technique
77/13. Group decision support systems
78/14. Idea board
79/15. Idea triggers
80/16. Innovation committee
81/17. Intercompany innovation groups
82/18. Lion's den
83/19. Lotus blossom technique, or the MY method
84/20. Mitsubishi brainstorming method
85/21. Morphological analysis
86/22. NHK method
87/23. Nominal group technique
88/24. Phillips 66 (Discussion 66)
89/25. Photo-excursion
90/26. Pin card technique
91/27. Scenario writing
92/28. SIL method
93/29. Storyboarding
94/30. Synectics
95/31. Take five
96/32. TKJ method

CHOICE (Discussed in Chapter 6)
97/1. Dot voting
98/2. Screening matrix for ideas

IMPLEMENTATION (Discussed in Chapter 6)
99/1. Be a warrior
100/2. Force field analysis
101/3. How-how diagram

CONTROL (Described in Chapter 6 as part of environmental analysis and problem recognition)

REFERENCES

[1] This discussion is based on several sources. For example see: E. Frank Harrison, *The Managerial Decision Making Process*, 3rd ed. (Boston: Houghton Mifflin Company, 1987); Arthur B. VanGundy, *Creative Problem Solving: A Guide for Trainers and Management* (New York: Quorum Books, 1987); Carl E. Gregory, *The Management of Intelligence* (New York: McGraw-Hill, 1962); Charles Kepner and Benjamin Tregoe, *The Rational Manager* (New York: McGraw-Hill, 1965).

[2] James M. Higgins and Julian W. Vincze, *Strategic Management: Text and Cases, 5th ed.* (Ft. Worth, Tex.: Dryden Press, 1993), Chapters 1 and 3.

[3] Christopher Knowlton, "Shell Gets Rich by Beating Risk," *Fortune* (August 26, 1991), pp. 78–82; Adrienne Lisenmeyer, "Shell's Crystall Ball," *Financial World* (April 16, 1991), pp. 58–63.

[4] David A. Cowan, "Developing a Process Model of Problem Recognition," *Academy of Management Review* (October 1986), pp. 763-776.

[5] Karen Lowry Miller, "The Factory Guru Tinkering With Toyota," *Business Week* (May 17, 1993), pp. 95, 97.

[6] Charles Kepner and Benjamin Tregoe, *The New Rational Manager* (New York: McGraw-Hill, 1989); Cowan, op. cit.

[7] Ibid. for the first six items. The seventh is aimed at opportunity recognition and identification.

[8] Steven Levy, "Newton Rising," *Macworld* (February 1993), pp. 77, 80; Kathy Rebello, "'The Great Digital Hope' Could Be a Heartbreaker," *Business Week* (November 30, 1992), pp. 94–95.

[9] Karen Lowry Miller, "55 Miles Per Gallon: How Honda Did It," *Business Week* (September 23, 1991), pp. 82–83.

[10] Lois Therrien, "McRisky," *Business Week* (October 21, 1991), pp. 114–122.

[11] Alecia Swasy, "Kimberly-Clark Bets, Wins on Innovation," *Wall Street Journal* (November 22, 1991), p. A5.

[12] My discussion with a General Mills Restaurants Vice President.

[13] Martha T. Moore, "Sorting Out a Mess," *USA Today* (April 10, 1992), p. 5B.

[14] Trish Hall, "When Budding MBAs Try to Save Kool-Aid, Original Ideas are Scarce," *Wall Street Journal* (November 25, 1986), p. 31.

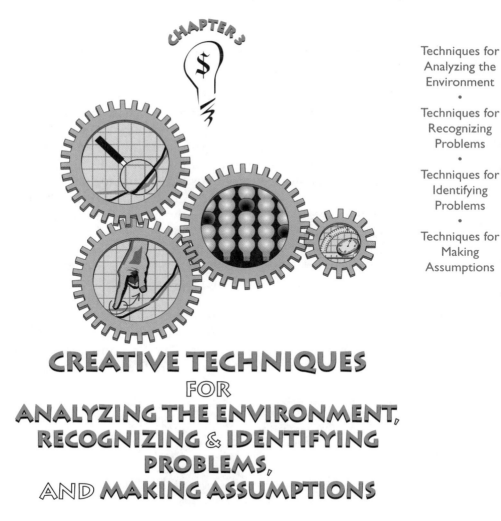

Techniques for
Analyzing the
Environment
•
Techniques for
Recognizing
Problems
•
Techniques for
Identifying
Problems
•
Techniques for
Making
Assumptions

CREATIVE TECHNIQUES
FOR
ANALYZING THE ENVIRONMENT,
RECOGNIZING & IDENTIFYING
PROBLEMS,
AND MAKING ASSUMPTIONS

Research shows creativity can be taught and companies are listening.
— Business Week

One of the best ways of becoming more creative is to use techniques (processes) that increase the potential for creativity in a given situation. Such techniques can be applied at all stages of the CPS process: analyzing the environment, recognizing the problem, identifying the problem, making assumptions, generating alternatives, choosing among alternatives, implementing the chosen solution and control. Many of these techniques involve the use of groups, which have been shown to be useful in raising levels of creativity. This book focuses on techniques used in generating alternatives but presents a few techniques for each of these other stages.

101
CREATIVE
PROBLEM
SOLVING
TECHNIQUES

This book discusses creative techniques and for the most part, leaves the standard rational techniques to other books.

The processes discussed in this chapter and ensuing ones were listed in Table 2.1. This chapter discusses the processes used in creatively analyzing the environment, recognizing and identifying problems and opportunities, and in making assumptions. Chapters 4 and 5 discuss techniques for generating creative alternatives. Chapter 4 focuses on individual techniques, Chapter 5 on group techniques. Chapter 6 reviews creative approaches to choice, implementation and control. The lengthier discussions in these chapters focus on the best-known, more difficult to understand, or most often used techniques. For longer and/or more complicated techniques, a summary of the steps necessary appears at the end of the discussion of that technique. In this and other chapters, techniques are presented in alphabetical order within sections to make them easier to find. Remember that techniques are numbered twice. The first number denotes the technique's position from 1 to 101, the second number is the technique's position within that section of the problem solving module.

TECHNIQUES FOR ANALYZING THE ENVIRONMENT

You can't solve a problem or take advantage of an opportunity until you know it exists. You can't be creative in generating alternatives until you have a reason to do so. The rational techniques for environmental analysis focus on standard control processes and environmental scanning. The following are recent, more creative approaches to environmental analysis.

1/1. COMPARISON AGAINST OTHERS: BENCHMARKING, BEST PRACTICES, AND RACING AGAINST PHANTOM COMPETITORS

Recently firms have turned to benchmarking as created by Xerox, together with the GE version of this technique, known as best practices, to identify potential problems. In benchmarking a firm compares its practices with those of the firm that is considered the best in its industry. In best practices, a firm compares itself with the firm that is considered the best at certain practices, regardless of the industry in which it operates. The results of these comparisons are used to motivate change and as goals for improvement.[1] When he was head of the Bonneville Power Administration, Peter T. Johnson created a fictitious supercompetitor with which to compare his organization.[2] Other firms create a composite supercompetitor, taking the best practices in different areas and combining them.

FIRM A.

2/2. HIRE FUTURISTS AND OTHER CONSULTANTS

No one says you have to discover problems yourself. Why not hire someone to perform this task for you? There are numerous futurists and other consultants who can guide you. They often bring a fresh perspective. For example, they may be able to see the forest for the trees, something someone close to the situation may not be able to do.

3/3. MONITOR WEAK SIGNALS

A standard strategic planning technique is to pay careful attention to weak signals in the market. Forecasters, clipping services, and networks can keep you informed. Attending seminars can perform a similar function. Two real estate developers decided to dispose of their prominent real estate holdings on the basis of weak signals just prior to the 1990–1992 recession. They used the funds generated by these sales to buy bankrupt or market depressed properties that became available during the recession.

4/4. OPPORTUNITY SEARCHES

Active opportunity searches can turn up new situations and new applications of current knowledge. You don't have to be limited to traditional sources. Try something new, like the manager who searches science fiction literature to find ideas that are applicable to his high-tech business. Try simply reading about new trends and asking what this means to your business.

TECHNIQUES FOR RECOGNIZING PROBLEMS

Many people recognize that a problem exists when they have failed to meet an objective or believe they may fail to meet an objective. The purpose of most control reports is to provide such comparisons. People may recognize an opportunity when they become aware that they could exceed their objectives by choosing a certain alternative or taking advantage of a situation.

Frequently individuals compare current performance with prior objectives, prior experience, or last year's performance in order to determine whether a problem exists. When they see a difference between the current situation and what was previously thought appropriate, they recognize that a problem exists.[3]

Fully describing current conditions is another way of being able to recognize a problem or opportunity. Simply review-

PROBLEM RECOGNITION LEADS TO NEW SOLUTIONS AT CONTINENTAL BANK

When Continental Bank Chairman Thomas Theobald created the Bank for Business strategy, he realized that its success would depend on having killer closers — officers who can actually close a deal. Recognition of this need prompted the bank to rethink its recruitment strategy. The revamped approach has been successful in meeting that goal, but it also has entailed making some significant changes. Although the new approach is costlier due to higher base salaries, the bank expects to offset those costs through long-term savings and increased revenue generation. After several meetings with psychologists, senior line management, and human resources staff, 6 skills were isolated that were believed to be a critical necessity for candidates: 1. analytical skills, 2. self-confidence, 3. creative problem-solving skills, 4. the ability to deal with ambiguity, 5. strong interpersonal skills, and 6. the ability to be proactive in transactions. Once the skills were identified, the bank incorporated them into its college recruiting evaluation form and included questions that would prompt interviewers.

Source: Todd S. Nelson, "Continental Banks on New Hiring Plan," *Personnel Journal*, November 1990, pp. 95-97.

THE INNOVATIVE EDGE IN ACTION 3.1

ing the existing situation may provide some insight into problems or potential problems. This seems obvious, but few people actually do it. Creatively recognizing problems is important to solving a problem as The Innovative Edge in Action suggests.

The following paragraphs describe more creative techniques for recognizing problems. Some are traditional approaches; others are new twists on approaches you may already be familiar with. Several involve ways of analyzing the environment in search of opportunities.

5/1. CAMELOT

Create an idealized situation, a Camelot. Now compare it to the existing situation. What are the differences? Why do they exist? What problems or opportunities are suggested by the differences?[4]

6/2. CHECKLISTS

Using a checklist when examining a situation can be extremely beneficial. A number of checklists have been developed for this purpose. For example, in their book *That's a Great Idea*, Tony Husch and Linda Foust provide numerous checklists designed to improve situation analysis. Among other things, their checklists provide guidance in finding opportunities, recognizing certain problems, generating new-product ideas, generating promotional ideas, and evaluating ideas.[5] Other checklists include strategic audits which examine strategy, management audits which examine overall management actions, quality audits which examine quality compliance, and social audits which examine for socially responsible activities.[6] Finally, Arthur B. VanGundy has provided a Product Improvement Checklist.[7] By using the checklist to compare what could be done to a product to what currently exists, a manager can identify problems and opportunities. VanGundy's list can also be used to generate creative alternatives and is discussed in more detail in Chapter 4.

7/3. INVERSE BRAINSTORMING

Read the section on brainstorming at the beginning of Chapter 5. Inverse brainstorming is a variant of the approach described there. Whereas regular brainstorming begins with a problem and looks for a solution, inverse brainstorming begins with a situation and looks for potential problems, such as lack of motivation in the work force.[8] In other words, you take what appears to be a satisfactory situation and see what you can find wrong with it.

8/4. LIMERICKS AND PARODIES

Make up limericks and parodies about a situation. People can't resist poking fun, and when they do so, problems may be revealed. For example, one employee used the theme song from "The Music Man" to poke fun at managers in his organization. He rewrote the song along these lines: "Trouble. We've got trouble right here in River City. It starts with an m and ends with a t, it's management. Yes sir, trouble right here in River City." He secretly distributed copies of his song to his fellow employees and to top management. An investigation followed, and two especially bad managers were replaced.

9/5. LISTING COMPLAINTS

One effective way of uncovering problems is to have employees, customers, or other constituents brainstorm a list of complaints, either individually or in groups. (See Chapter 5 for a description of brainstorming.) Another version of this approach is to have employees list stumbling blocks that they have encountered.[9]

10/6. RESPONDING TO SOMEONE ELSE

Sometimes people bring you problems or opportunities that deserve careful consideration even if they seem farfetched. In some businesses this happens quite often. Stories abound of cases in which people have failed to recognize the potential of ideas brought to them by others. As noted in Chapter 1, George Lucas took the "Star Wars" idea to twelve movie studios before Fox decided to produce it. IBM, General Motors, and DuPont were all offered the xerography idea and rejected it as impossible and unnecessary. So Chester Carlson and his associates went into business for themselves and became multimillionaires. Victor Kiam was offered a chance to buy Velcro for $25,000 but failed to see its potential. Velcro applications were estimated to have had a total of $6 billion in sales from inception to 1988.[10]

The moral of these stores: Listen to others. Envision the possibilities.

11/7. ROLE PLAYING

Role playing requires you to pretend you are someone else. You may role play with another person in an interactive learning situation much like a play, or by simply imagining another person's situation and walking through it in your mind.

Putting yourself in someone else's shoes—for example, a customer's—may give you totally new insights into a situation. It may allow you to solve potential problems before they become real ones. Imagine that you are someone else in the problem situation. Describe the problem from that person's perspective. Now solve it from that perspective. What new insights did you gain?

12/8. SUGGESTION PROGRAMS

From the standpoint of the organization, the suggestion program offers a tremendous opportunity to learn about the existence of problems and to obtain some solutions. But such programs must be implemented effectively. Japanese firms have really good suggestion programs. Some U.S. firms, such as Lockheed, also have good programs. The Japanese take their programs seriously. Akio Morita, co-founder of Sony, comments on his firm's suggestion programs, "We insist that all our employees contribute their thoughts and ideas, not just their manual effort. We get an average of eight suggestions a year from each employee. We take most of these ideas seriously."[11]

13/9. WORKOUTS AND OTHER GROUP APPROACHES

GE has developed a process known as the workout. Workouts involve a three-day retreat in which managers and their subordinates gather to solve problems experienced by the work unit. It is a highly participative effort with a unique twist. Subordinates suggest the causes of the problems and recommend solutions. On the third day these are presented to their manager, whose superior manager is also in attendance sitting behind his or her subordinate but facing the employees. The workout manager must choose among three responses to subordinates' recommendations: Yes, no, or let's examine it and make a decision by a specific date. Deferrals are discouraged.[12] The workout manager must make a decision about employee suggestions without knowing what his or her boss's reactions are because of how the two managers are seated. Other group techniques (such as creativity circles, described in Chapter 5) can also be used to recognize problems. Simple group discussion may lead to both recognition and identification.

TECHNIQUES FOR
IDENTIFYING PROBLEMS

Identifying the problem means making certain that your actions will be directed toward solving the real problem or taking advantage of the real opportunity, rather than merely addressing symptoms of the problem or an apparent (but not necessarily real) opportunity. Problem identification requires careful analysis.

A well-known set of identification techniques has been suggested by Charles Kepner and Benjamin Tregoe, who believe that correctly identifying the problem is the most important step in creative problem solving. Their approach, described in their book *The Rational Manager*, begins by asking what's different now than before; this is followed by what, where, when, how, and why questions. Kepner and Tregoe like to use the example of a ball bearing manufacturing facility that began finding impurities in some of its ball bearings. The company replaced the machine that manufactured the ball bearings, but impurities continued to appear. Eventually, after answering the "when" question, the company's managers determined that the impurities occurred only at periodic intervals. After asking and answering the other questions, they discovered that an air-freshening unit was blowing impurities into the molten metal; the unit came on only at certain times during the day.[13] Finally, the real problem was identified.

This section describes twelve techniques that can be used in the problem identification stage of creative problem solving.

14/1. BOUNCE IT OFF SOMEONE ELSE

Simply talking to someone else about a problem employs the idea that "two heads are better than one." Suggest what you think the problem is and elicit the other person's reaction. Each of you can offer definitions and defend them until you find one that you can agree on.

15/2. CONSENSUS BUILDING

A large number of techniques for consensus building exist. Among these are voting in a democratic manner and sitting in a circle and discussing the problem until a consensus is reached. Creativity circles, described in Chapter 5, often begin by reaching a consensus definition of the problem.

16/3. DRAW A PICTURE OF THE PROBLEM

One way to make certain that you are identifying the real problem is to draw a picture of it. This process can also be used in generating alternatives. Because creativity is largely a right-brain function (in right-handed people, the opposite in left-handed people), and the right brain is more visually oriented than the left brain, (opposite for left-handers) drawing pictures seems to aid the creative process. If you can "see" the problem, you have a better chance of making certain that you are solving the real problem. So take out a pen and a piece of paper and draw a picture of your problem. What insights do you gain?

17/4. EXPERIENCE KIT

The experience kit was developed by IdeaScope of Cambridge, Massachusetts. It involves putting problem solvers through an experience that causes them to understand the problem better and therefore generate more and better solutions. It is a sort of combination of role playing and idea triggers. The experience kit involves participants in the problem. For example, IdeaScope provided detergent brand managers trying to improve their products' sales with an experience kit consisting of a sample of competitors' products; a diary for recording when the participants' own households did laundry in a week and how big the loads were; the requirement to visit a local laundry company (address provided) for at least one hour; and a dirty shirt that had to be washed at home using the company's product and then worn to the creativity session. Several of the spots on the shirts wouldn't come out. All of the experiences provided the brand managers with new insights into the problem.[14]

18/5. FISHBONE DIAGRAM

Two very useful approaches to identifying problems are the fishbone diagram and the related why-why diagram. (The latter will be discussed near the end of this chapter.) The fishbone diagram, sometimes referred to as the Ishikawa diagram, was developed by Professor Kaoru Ishikawa of the University of Tokyo.[15] The primary purpose of this exercise is to identify and list all the possible causes of the problem at hand. This is primarily a group problem identification technique, but it can be used by individuals as well.

This process is called the fishbone diagram because of the unique way in which the information gathered is arranged visually. When the problem and its causes are recorded, they form a diagram that resembles the skeleton of a fish. The problem is written down and enclosed in a circle on the right side of a sheet of paper. A straight line is drawn to the left and appears much like the backbone of a fish. (See Figure 3.1 for an abbreviated example of a fishbone diagram.) The next step involves drawing stems at a 45 degree angle to the backbone line. At the end of each of these stems are listed all of the causes of the problem that can be brainstormed. Additional stems may

Figure 3.1 FishBone Diagram

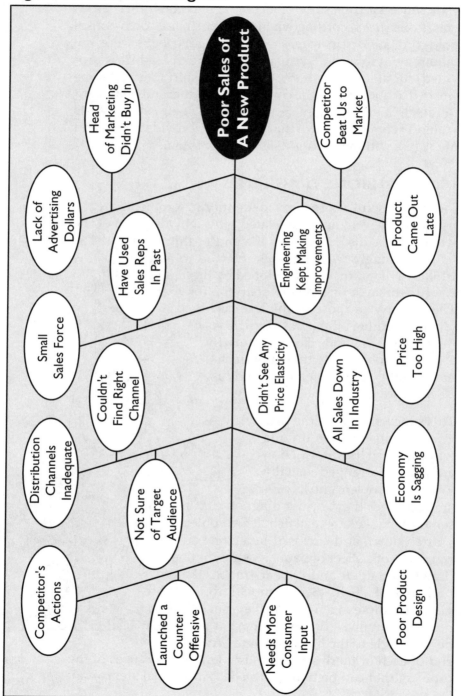

be added if necessary. Branches can be placed on each stem for further breakdowns of each cause. The causes should be listed with the least complicated nearest the head of the fish and the most complicated at the tail, with those in between listed on a continuum from least to most complicated.

The fishbone diagram can be brainstormed over more than one session. Ishikawa describes the process as one in which "you write your problem down on the head of the fish and then let it cook overnight." If the technique is employed over two or more sessions, new ideas may arise from three main effects: (1) There is time for the subconscious to work on the problem; (2) participants are likely to be less inhibited as the authorship of particular contributions will be forgotten; and (3) people may become more immersed in the problem if they think about it day and night.

When the diagram is completed, the individual or group begins to analyze the stems and the branches to determine the real problem or problems that need to be solved. If simpler problems are examined first, they can be removed from consideration before more complicated problems are tackled. If the problem solver(s) decide that certain causes are more significant than others, these will be given more attention in the alternative generation stage of CPS.

The fishbone diagram is extremely useful for identifying problems for several reasons:

1. It encourages problem solvers to study all parts of a problem before making a decision.

2. It helps show the relationships between causes and the relative importance of those causes.

3. It helps start the creative process because it focuses the problem solver(s) on the problem.

4. It helps start a logical sequence for solving a problem.

5. It helps problem solvers see the total problem as opposed to focusing on a narrow part of it.

6. It offers a way to reduce the scope of the problem and solve less complex issues rather than more complex ones.

7. It helps keep people focused on the real problem rather than going off on tangents.

When you first use the fishbone diagram, begin with small, readily definable problems and move to more complex issues as you learn the process.

SUMMARY OF STEPS

1. Write down the problem and enclose it in a circle on the right side of the paper.
2. Draw a straight line to the left; this is the "backbone."
3. Draw stems at a 45 degree angle from the backbone.
4. Brainstorm all the causes of the problem and place them at the end of each of the stems.
5. Draw additional stems and substems as necessary.
6. List more complicated causes at the tail of the fish and less complicated ones at the head of the fish.

19/6. KING OF THE MOUNTAIN

King of the mountain is a children's game in which one player gets on top of something, such as a stump or a chair, and the others try to knock him or her off. A similar game can be used as a problem identification technique.[16] One or two individuals take a position on what the problem is, and other members of the group attempt to knock them off their definitional "mountain." To succeed in doing so, the challenger must have a better definition of the problem. Just as in the game, once someone has knocked another person off the mountain, he or she must get on top of the mountain. His or her ideas are then attacked until another challenger succeeds in becoming "king of the mountain." The survivor, who might have modified any of the ideas presented earlier, possesses what is now a group consensus regarding the true nature of the problem.

20/7. REDEFINING A PROBLEM OR OPPORTUNITY

Redefine a problem in as many ways as you possibly can. Perhaps this will help you see it in another light. Imagine it from the perspective of someone who is less familiar with it. Say the new definition aloud. Perhaps you'll hear something

48

in what you're saying that you haven't noticed before. Try to determine how you feel about it. Pretend that you don't know what the problem is but do know some of the variables involved. If you were a member of another profession, how would you view the problem? How many different ways can you express this problem or opportunity? Now go back and examine what you have done. Do you see the problem any differently?

The following exercise can get you started in applying this technique. Think of a problem or opportunity and restate it five different ways:

1. _____

2. _____

3. _____

4. _____

5. _____

21/8. REWRITE OBJECTIVES IN DIFFERENT WAYS

In order to make certain that you are really addressing the underlying problem, you can rewrite your objectives or other criteria in several different ways. For example, if your problem is to increase productivity, this might be restated as: increase sales per employee, cut costs, how do I increase productivity, be more efficient, be more effective, set better goals, and so on.

22/9. SQUEEZE AND STRETCH

As part of the problem-solving process, you can try "squeezing" and "stretching" the problem.[17] Thinking in terms of squeezing and stretching allows you to analyze a problem better. You squeeze a problem to find its basic components. You stretch the problem in order to discover more of its scope. Stretching a problem allows you to see how much there really is to it and what other facts relate to it.

To squeeze a problem, ask a chain of questions beginning with the word "why."

Example:	
Question:	*Why am I doing this?*
Answer:	Because I want to.
Question:	*Why do I want to?*
Answer:	Because I have been told to by my boss.
Question:	*Why does my boss want me to do it?*
Answer:	Because her boss wants her to do it.

To stretch a problem, ask a chain of questions beginning with the word "what."

Example	
Question:	*What is this problem about?*
Answer:	Learning financial analysis.
Question:	*What is financial analysis all about?*
Answer:	Accounting and relationships among accounts.
Question:	*What is learning all about?*
Answer:	Discovery, developing, etc.
Question:	*What is accounting all about?*
Answer:	Giving meaning to the transactions of an organization.

Continue with these processes until you have a better understanding of the problems.

23/10. WHAT DO YOU KNOW?

Once you recognize that a problem exists, simply writing down what you know about it might help. List all the characteristics of the situation. What suspicions do you have? What kind of evidence do you have to justify those suspicions, and how good is it? What did you learn?

24/11. WHAT PATTERNS EXIST?

Look at the available information. Do you see any patterns or relationships, causal or otherwise? Draw a diagram showing the interconnections among the facts you have uncovered. Japanese managers frequently use diagrams to discuss problems. Their use of visual aids often helps them simplify complex situations. Visual representations help stimulate not only insight but creativity as well. So give diagrams a try.

25/12. WHY-WHY DIAGRAM

This technique is a variation of the approach used in the fishbone diagram. It is used to identify the cause(s) of a problem in a systematic way.[18] This diagram generally moves from left to right, with the problem statement on the left-hand side. (See Figure 3.2 for an abbreviated example of a why-why diagram.) There is no backbone; instead, this diagram is designed more like a traditional decision tree with component stems identified to the right of the problem statement. Branches may also be identified to the right of each stem. One moves from the problem statement to the stems and branches by asking the question "Why?"

For example, as shown in Figure 3.2 , if the problem is "New Product Sales Are Poor" and you ask why, five possible causes emerge: poor product design, inadequate promotion, ineffective distribution, too high a price, and failure to identify target market. Possible causes of each of

Figure 3.2 Why-Why Diagram

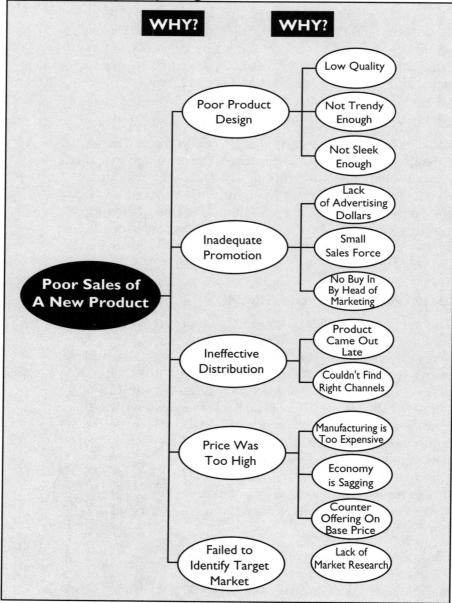

these can be identified by the question "Why?" again. For example, a poor product design may be due to low quality, failure to recognize trends in consumer tastes, or aesthetic factors ("not sleek enough").

This technique offers many of the same benefits as the fishbone diagram. In particular, it helps problem solvers explore many more possible causes and relate them to the overall problem, rather than focusing on a single narrow cause. In fact, the why-why diagram probably leads to a more thorough analysis than the fishbone diagram. Notice the differences between Figures 3.1 and 3.2. The latter is a more rational layout of problems along the more traditional lines of the marketing mix— product, promotion, price, distribution, and target market.

SUMMARY OF STEPS

1. State the problem on the left side of the paper.
2. Create a typical decision tree of causes to the right of the problem by asking a succession of "whys" regarding the problem and each of the possible causes.
3. Continue this process until a sufficient level of detail has been achieved.

PROBLEM STATEMENT

At the end of the problem identification stage, by using the various techniques described here, in addition to more traditional analytical approaches, you should have identified the causal problem and be able to make a more accurate problem statement than you might have otherwise.

Various approaches to stating the problem exist. Generally, the more specific the problem can be stated, the easier it will be to solve that problem. Thus if the problem in Figure 3.2 is stated as "poor product partly due to poor quality" this would not be as effective as if the problem were stated as "poor quality due to poor workmanship caused by poor worker training."[19] Some CPS authors believe that the problem should always be stated in terms of the preposition "to" followed by some object and an action verb. An example would be, "to improve worker training on chip making machines in order to improve product quality to satisfactory levels."

TECHNIQUES FOR MAKING ASSUMPTIONS

Assumptions about the future underlie every decision you make. Assumptions set constraints on your solutions. People frequently force solutions into the shape they want by manipulating the underlying assumptions. One man entered the restaurant business after hours of computer spreadsheet manipulations, assuming that the revenues would be sufficient to justify the investment. Two years later he was out of business. His assumptions about sales were wrong, as were his assumptions about food costs and his own ability to motivate low-wage workers.

I know of only one creative technique for making assumptions. It's called assumption reversal.

26/1. ASSUMPTION REVERSAL

List all your assumptions about the problem. Now reverse them and try to solve the problem.[20] You aren't looking for a real solution to the newly stated problem so much as you are trying to recognize the limitations of the solutions you come up with when you use your original assumptions.

You can also use this process to get new ideas for solving the original problem. Sometimes you can use it just to get new ideas.

Suppose that your problem is to gain additional market share. The original assumptions are that another firm is dominant, you can buy market share through advertising, and you have a superior product or service that no one really knows about.

Now reverse those assumptions. No firm is dominant, advertising doesn't seem to help, and you have an inferior product that everybody knows is inferior. What are you going to do?

FEDERAL EXPRESS: SORTING OUT A MESS

In the spring of 1992, Federal Express faced a major problem. As many as 4,300 packages a month were still missing their flights, even though additional employees had been assigned to the "minisort"—the frenzied last effort to get packages on their assigned flights each night. Because the company "absolutely, positively" guarantees overnight delivery, the packages that missed their flights had to be put on commerical flights at a cost of $16.60 per package. The company was spending $875,000 a year just to ship packages that had missed their flights. A team of twelve minisort workers was chosen to solve this problem.

A manager, Melvin Washington, headed the team, but he served primarily as a facilitator. The team met mostly on its own time, usually over breakfast, after spending long hours sorting packages on the night shift. The team interviewed many fellow employees, managers of other divisions, and staff personnel and discussed numerous possible problem areas. They used a four-step creative problem-solving technique that Federal Express had taught them in conjunction with a total quality management program.

After many hours of hard work, the team determined that several factors were contributing to the problem. First, there were too many people working on the minisort, which only added to the confusion. Second, many of those workers didn't know what they were supposed to do. The team recommended that the number of minisort workers be reduced from 150 to 80 and that steps be taken to improve workers' understanding of their tasks. For example, sorting codes had been relatively easy to memorize in the beginning, but as the firm had grown, more and more codes had been added, making memorization impossible. The team recommended that codes be posted so that workers could see them.

CONTINUES ON PAGE 56

THE INNOVATIVE EDGE IN ACTION 3.2

FEDERAL EXPRESS
Continued from page 53

They also worked with other sorting departments to increase their quality control efforts, thereby reducing the number of packages sent to the nightly minisort. Finally, a "traffic cop" was appointed to direct the tractors carrying sorted packages to the right planes.

The results were impressive. The time spent on minisort dropped from more than an hour a night to 38 minutes. In one year, the number of packages missing their flights fell to about 1,800 a month. The firm saved $938,000 in eighteen months. "It seems so simple," Washington observes, "but it wasn't. The hardest part was selling it to everyone." The team members were pleased with their solutions, even though what they proposed ended up costing each of them about $50 a week in lost wages because their work hours were reduced.

Source: Martha T. Moore, "Sorting Out a Mess," *USA Today* (April 10, 1992), p. 5B.

It's obvious that your responses to the second set of assumptions will differ from your responses to the first set. What new solutions do you come up with? In what ways can these be applied to the original problem?

Give it a try.

ANALYZING THE ENVIRONMENT, RECOGNIZING AND IDENTIFYING THE PROBLEM, & MAKING ASSUMPTIONS

The techniques listed in this chapter are some of the more creative approaches to these three stages of problem solving. Many are specifically designed to enhance creativity in these stages. The importance of creative activity in these stages is demonstrated by the Federal Express example described in The Innovative Edge in Action 3.2.

REFERENCES

[1] Otis Port and Geoffrey Smith, "Beg, Borrow — And Benchmark," *Business Week* (November 30, 1992), pp. 74–75; Thomas A. Stewart, "GE Keeps Those Ideas Coming," *Fortune* (August 12, 1991), pp. 41–49.

[2] Peter T. Johnson, "Why I Race Against Phantom Competitors," *Harvard Business Review* (September/October 1988), pp. 106–112.

[3] William F. Pounds, "The Process of Problem Finding," *Industrial Management Review*, Fall 1969, pp. 1-9.

[4] Kent Seltzman, an MBA student of mine, suggested this process and limericks and parodies which follow.

[5] Tony Husch and Linda Foust, *That's a Great Idea*, (Berkeley, CA: 10 Speed Press, 1987).

[6] James M. Higgins and Julian W. Vincze, *Strategic Management: Text and Cases*, 5th ed., (Ft. Worth, Tex.: The Dryden Press, 1993), Chapter 10.

[7] Arthur B. VanGundy, *The Product Improvement Checklist (PICL™)* (Point Pleasant, N.J.: Point Publishing, 1985).

[8] "Creative Group Techniques," *Small Business Report* (September 1984), pp. 52-57.

[9] Anne Skagen, "Creativity Tools: Versatile Problem Solvers That Can Double as Fun and Games," *Supervisory Management* (October 1991), pp. 1–2.

[10] Victor Kiam, speech to the Roy E. Crummer Graduate School of Business, Rollins College, Winter Park, Florida (October 28, 1985); Judith Stone, "Velcro: The Final Frontier," *Discover* (May 1988), pp. 82–84.

[11] Akito Mortia with Edwin M. Reingold and Mitsuko Shinonrma, "Made in Japan," *Macmillan Executive Summary Program* (1, 1987), p. 1.

[12] Thomas A. Stewart, loc. cit.

[13] Charles Kepner and Benjamin Tregoe, *The Rational Manager*, (New York: McGraw-Hill, 1967).

[14] Bryan W. Mattimore, "Brainstormer's Boot Camp," *Success* (October 1991), pp. 22, 24.

[15] As described in Simon Majaro, *The Creative Gap: Managing Ideas for Profit* (London: Longman, 1988) pp. 133-137.

[16] Dan Koberg and Jim Bagnall, *Universal Traveler* (Los Altos, CA: William Kaufman, Inc., 1974), p. 57.

[17] Ibid., p. 63.

[18] Simon Majaro, op. cit.; pp. 137 - 138.

[19] Ibid., p. 139.

[20] Michael Michalko, *Thinkertoys* (Berkeley, CA: 10 Speed Press, 1992), pp.43-49.

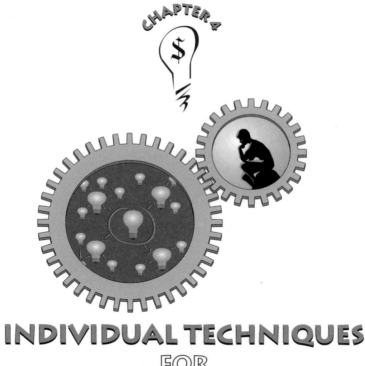

Individual
Processes for
Generating
Creative
Alternatives
•
A Quick
Guide to
My Favorite
Techniques

INDIVIDUAL TECHNIQUES
FOR
GENERATING ALTERNATIVES

*Creativity is necessary for survival in today's environment. All hotels,
once you get outside of the truly five-star hotels of the world, are the
same; the product varies only in the color of the lobby. To survive,
innovation is the key.*

—Michael Leven
Former President
Days Inns

One of the easiest and quickest ways of increasing the level
of innovation in an organization is to develop its members'
skills in generating alternatives as part of the problem-solving
process. There is nothing particularly "mystical" about these
skills. People tend to think that having really good ideas is
possible for only a few, and that the rest of us, who don't
have special "intuitive" talents, cannot be creative. Nothing
could be further from the truth. This chapter and the next
one present a large number of creative techniques for generating alternatives. Some may be utilized by individuals, others by work groups, many by both. These techniques will
produce results quickly and easily for virtually anyone who
is willing to take the time to learn them and use them.

When applied to problem solving within an appropriate organizational culture, these processes can help an organization solve its problems more effectively than its competitors, including the problem of how to obtain a sustainable competitive advantage. Firms such as Frito-Lay, Xerox, and 3M provide extensive training in these processes and attribute substantial profits to their utilization by managers, professional staff, and other employees.[1]

A positive feature of most of the techniques described in this chapter is their appeal to individuals with an analytical bent as well as to those with an intuitive orientation. Most of these processes rely on step-by-step procedures that fit readily into the rational problem-solving models used by most managers, professional staff, and other organizational problem solvers. Even those that at first seem entirely intuitive, such as the excursion technique (one of my ten favorite processes), when practiced by analytically as well as intuitively oriented people, will quickly reveal their value.

Every individual is likely to feel more comfortable with certain techniques than with others. In part this stems from the types of problems that a person faces most frequently and is also a function of personality characteristics such as problem-solving style. For example, I have used these eight processes:

27/1.	Analogies and metaphors
29/3.	Association
37/11.	Direct analogies
47/21.	Mind mapping
51/25.	Personal analogies
53/27.	Product improvement checklist
57/31.	Rolling in the grass of ideas
62/36.	Verbal checklist for creativity

(both personally and with clients) much more than the others, but I have used almost all of them at one time or another. Your personal preferences and problem-solving situations will help guide your choices. Table 4.5, at the end of the chapter, contains a quick guide to my favorite individual and group alternative generation processes.

INDIVIDUAL PROCESSES FOR GENERATING CREATIVE ALTERNATIVES

This chapter describes thirty-eight processes that can be used by individuals to generate creative alternatives. Some of these techniques can be used by groups as well. However, Chapter 5 describes the major techniques that can be used by groups, some of which can also be used by individuals. Most of the processes described in these two chapters can be used in various situations, but a few are appropriate only for specific types of problems. Descriptions of the more frequently used processes note such limitations where they exist.

27/1. ANALOGIES AND METAPHORS

Analogies and metaphors can serve as a means of identifying problems and understanding them better. They may also be used to generate alternative solutions. Often you can draw an analogy between your problem and something else, or express it in metaphorical terms. These may provide insight into how to solve the problem.

Analogies

An analogy is a comparison of two things that are essentially dissimilar but are shown through the analogy to have some similarity. Analogies are often used to solve problems. For example, when NASA found it necessary to design a satellite that would be tethered to a space station by a thin wire sixty miles long, it realized that the motion of reeling it in would cause it to act like a pendulum with an ever-widening arc. Stanford scientist Thomas Kane, using the analogy of a yo-yo, determined that a small electric motor on the satellite would allow it to crawl back up the tether to the space station.[2] A product development team from Atlas Copco Roc Tec, a mining-equipment company based in Golden, Colorado, used analogies to develop a machine that would both dig ore and load it onto a conveyor belt. One of the members of the problem-solving team was an entomologist. He suggested the praying mantis as an example. As it eats, it clutches food between its forelegs and thrusts it into its mouth. The result of this analogy was the ROC 302, a large tractor with shovels on each side (like forelegs) that load ore onto a conveyor belt running through the middle of the machine.[3] As these examples demonstrate, while in its simplest form an analogy is a comparison of dissimilar entities, in many instances analogies are fully developed comparisons, more intricate and detailed than a metaphor or a simile.

Metaphors

A metaphor is a figure of speech in which two different universes of thought are linked by some point of similarity. In the broadest sense of the term, all metaphors are simple analogies, but not all analogies are metaphors. Typically, metaphors treat one thing as if it were something else so that a resemblance that would not ordinarily be perceived is pointed out. Examples include the idea drought, frozen wages, the corporate battleground, liquid assets. Also: The sergeant barks an order, the cold wind cuts to the bone, the road was a ribbon of moonlight. Metaphors have many uses in creative endeavors. For example, they have been used in sales to create new ways of viewing old realities.[4] Hiroo Wantanabe, a project team leader for Honda, coined the following metaphor to describe his team's tremendous challenge: Theory of Automobile Evoluation, 'If a car could indeed evolve like a living organism, how should it evolve?' he asked his team. This thought process eventually led them to the very successful Honda City model.[5]

Comparisons that are obvious are not metaphors. To say that the noise of firecrackers on the Fourth of July sounds like gunfire, for example, is not a metaphor. Metaphors occur when a surprisingly imaginative connection is made between two different ideas or images that are normally perceived as dissimilar.

Think of five metaphors that describe the meaning of life, such as "life is a maze."

1. _____

2. _____

3. _____

4. _____

5. _____

Now think of a problem. Write five metaphors that describe your problem.

1. _____

2. _____

3. _____

4. _____

5. _____

For each of the metaphors you have listed, ask yourself what insights it provides into how to solve your problem. What solutions do your metaphors suggest?

Similes

Similes are specific types of metaphors that use the words "like" and "as"—for example, the wind cut like a knife, his hand was as quick as a frog's tongue. They too can be used to suggest comparisons that offer solutions.

SUMMARY OF STEPS

1. Think of an analogy between your problem and something else.
2. Ask yourself what insights or potential solutions the analogy suggests.

28/2. ANALYSIS OF PAST SOLUTIONS

Technical reports, professional reports, and books telling how others have solved problems can be employed to determine possible solutions for a problem. Even if the ways in which a problem has been solved in the past are not exactly suited to your situation, you can adapt them on the basis of your own experience.

29/3. ASSOCIATION

Association involves making a mental connection between two objects or ideas. It works through three primary laws originally laid down by the ancient Greeks: contiguity, similarity, and contrast.[6] Contiguity means nearness—for example, when you see a chalkboard you are reminded of school. Similarity means that one object or thought will remind you of a similar object or thought. For example, when you see a Ford Taurus you might think of a Mercury Sable. Metaphors and analogies depend on similarity. Contrast refers to dissimilarities that are nearly opposites—black/white, man/woman, child/adult. Thus, association involves thinking of something near, similar to, or in contrast to the object or idea in question.

Free Association

In free association, you say whatever comes into your mind relative to a word you just wrote or relative to a one- or two-word definition of a problem. A trail of thoughts is pursued in this way. Free association is a good group exercise as well as an individual one. The purpose is simply to get thoughts onto a whiteboard or sheet of paper that will trigger new thoughts about the problem. You don't expect to find solutions per se; rather, you are looking for thoughts that might lead to solutions. For example, on one occasion a group of bank managers started free associating on the word "fast." "Fox" and "jet plane" were among the associations that resulted; so was "Federal Express." "Federal Express," in turn, led the group to think of bar codes and optical scanners, which were perceived as a possible solution to the problem: differentiating among home equity loans. The bar codes could be used to inform customers of the status of the loan at any point in the approval process. Later the bank instituted 24-hour approvals for home equity loans, which left this solution without a problem, but the free-association technique had been used effectively.

At Campbell Soup Company, product developers began by randomly selecting the word "handle" from a dictionary. (Organized random search is described later in this chapter.) Through free association the word "utensil" was suggested. This led to "fork." One participant joked about a soup that could be eaten with a fork. The group reasoned that you couldn't eat soup with a fork unless it was thick with vegetables and meat ... and Campbell's Chunky Soups, an extremely successful product line, was born.[7]

Now try free associating, starting with a one-word summary of your problem on line 1. On line 2, write down the first word that comes to mind after looking at line 1. On line 3, write down the first word that comes to mind after looking at line 2. Continue until you have ten words. (Twenty to thirty is even better.)

1. _____   1a._____

2. _____   2a._____

3. _____   3a._____

4. _____   4a._____

5. _____   5a._____

6. _____   6a._____

7. _____   7a._____

8. _____   8a._____

9. _____   9a._____

10. _____   10a._____

Now look at these ten words. See how each of them gives you some insight into your problem. Can you use any to draw analogies that could lead to solutions? Take the words that grab you and use them to brainstorm solutions, or use them to form new associations that can then be used to brainstorm solutions. Write your ideas on lines 1a through 10a.

Creativity consultant Roger von Oech used names of celebrities to trigger ideas. The problem was to develop icons for a new software package. When Vanna White's name was introduced, the group thought first of letter turning, then pretty women, and finally, for some reason, airhead. Bingo! The new icon was a vacuum cleaner for a function that collected something from one place and put it somewhere else.[8]

Regular Association

The difference between free association and regular association is that in regular association, the associated word must somehow be related to the word before it. Thus, "airplane" could lead to "pilot" but not to "tree." In free association, in contrast, any word, the first word that pops into your mind, can be used.

SUMMARY OF STEPS

1. Write down a word (or two) that may or may not represent your problem or some aspect of it.
2. Write down whatever word comes to mind relative to this word.
3. After completing a series of such associations, study the words to see if any of them lead to insights or solutions to your problem.

30/4. ATTRIBUTE ASSOCIATION CHAINS

As in attribute listing, this technique begins with a list of the attributes of a problem. But instead of analytically changing the attributes as you would in attribute listing, you free associate on each attribute to generate ideas about the problem.[9]

For example, suppose that the problem is to improve on the phonograph record as a device for carrying music. You begin by listing the attributes of the record—its size, weight, color, composition, cost, and so on. If you free associated on these attributes, you might look for ways to reduce the weight of the device or cut its cost or change its composition. If you free associated on aspects of composition, you might come up with words like: "computers," "change," "lasers," "fiber optics," and so on. Eventually, you might develope the cassette tape or the compact disc.

Like many of the techniques discussed in this book, this one depends on your ability to let your mind go (in this case, to free associate) and to come up with ideas based on thoughts that are seemingly unrelated. You have to be able to envision how the results might be applied to the problem. For example, in the case of devices for carrying music, you need to be able to envision how the application of "computers" or "lasers" would lead to a new device such as the compact disc.

SUMMARY OF STEPS

1. List all the attributes or qualities of a problem or object.
2. Free associate on each attribute or group of attributes to generate solutions to or insights into the problem or object.
3. Study the suggested solutions to determine which one is most feasible.
4. Examine the remaining associated words to determine what solutions they suggest, and then determine which of these is most feasible.

31/5. ATTRIBUTE LISTING

The technique of attribute listing, developed by Professor Robert Platt Crawford of the University of Nebraska, consists of listing all the attributes or qualities of a problem or object.[10] Then the problem solver systematically analyzes each attribute or group of attributes and attempts to change them in as many ways as possible. Examples of attributes include physical attributes, such as color, speed, odor, weight, size, and mass; social attributes, such as norms, taboos, responsibilities, leadership, and communication; psychological attributes, such as perception, motivation, appearance, symbolism, self-image, and needs; and other attributes such as cost, function, length of service, and so on. The application of this technique to a common lead pencil is illustrated in Table 4.1. Although most of the ideas shown are not new and some aren't very practical, they offer some interesting possibilities.

TABLE 4.1 Example of Attribute Listing

ATTRIBUTE	POSSIBLE CHANGES
Lead produces writing.	Light might be used to affect photographic paper.
	Heat might be used to affect a special paper. Could use a solution.
	Instead of solid lead might use a chemical solution that reacted with the paper (some of these variations might lead to a pencil or writing instrument that never has to be sharpened or refilled).
Wooden casing.	Could be metal; plastic; entirely made of graphite.
Plain yellow color.	Could be any color; carry advertising; or have a design (perhaps women would buy pens and pencils carrying the same design as their dresses).

Source: Charles S. Whiting, "Operational Techniques of Creative Thinking," *Advanced Management*, October 1955, p.26.

SUMMARY OF STEPS

1. List all the attributes or qualities of a problem or object.
2. Systematically analyze each attribute or group of attributes and attempt to change it in as many ways as possible.
3. Review the resulting attributes for the best solutions.

32/6 BACK TO THE CUSTOMER

Turning our attention from production problems to marketing problems, we can consider how what we do relates to the customer in terms of product, price, promotion, distribution, and target market. As an exercise, below each of the following headings write the key related issues you should consider in going "back to the customer" to solve your problem. This means that you would identify issues for each of the five marketing mix factors related to the problem. Then identify solutions for each of these issues.

PRODUCT: _____

_____

_____

_____

PRICE: _____

_____

_____

_____

PROMOTION: _____

_____

_____

_____

DISTRIBUTION: _____

_____

_____

_____

TARGET MARKET: _____

_____

_____

_____

What insights did you gain? Do any of your entries remind you of something else? Do they lead to any new ideas?

SUMMARY OF STEPS

1. State your problem.
2. Identify the various product, price, promotion, distribution, and target market issues related to solving that problem in terms of how the customer would be affected.
3. From these, develop possible solutions.

33/7. BACK TO THE SUN

All physical things can be reduced to their energy equivalents. By tracing their history back to the natural resources from which they were developed, and ultimately to the sun as the source of all energy, we can better appreciate how the elements of a problem are related.[11] This better understanding may suggest solutions.

Suppose, for example, that we are trying to develop a shoe using different materials than those commonly used, or a different way of using existing materials in making shoes. When you look at a shoe you see leather, rubber, strings, nails, polish, thread, and so on. For each of these elements you can trace a process back to natural resources and ultimately to the sun.

RUBBER: stamps, mold, heel factories, shipping, raw latex process, rubber plant, rubber tree.

STRINGS: plastic tips, woven fabric, coloring, fiber, woven fiber, spun fiber, drawn fiber, plastic, petroleum, chemicals, fossil deposits.

LEATHER: texturing, coloring, hole punching, cutting out, tannery, slaughterhouse, trucking, ranch, feed.

POLISH: application, coloring, container, mixing, trucking, petroleum, chemicals, fossil deposits.

NAILS: hammer, forge, wire, spools, steel, Pittsburgh shipping, Minnesota iron, ore deposits.

Do any of these words suggest new materials or uses? For example, could rubber be stamped differently, colored differently? Could different fibers be used? Could strings be all plastic, not cloth, or made of something besides cloth or plastic? Could leather be made from something besides cowhide? Could the leather be a different color? Could polish be made from something other than chemicals? Looking at these words may trigger new thoughts.

34/8. CIRCLE OF OPPORTUNITY

This process consists of randomly selecting problem attributes and combining them to create a topic for a brainstorming session.[12] This process can be time-consuming but very rewarding in terms of ideas generated. The technique is somewhat similar to the attribute-listing and attribute association processes discussed previously, although it was developed independently. It also contains ingredients of other techniques, such as some of the forcing techniques. The sample to the right shows the attributes for a trade book. Such a circle was used in developing this book.

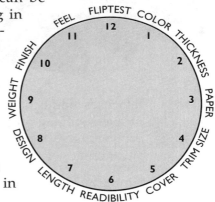

SUMMARY OF STEPS

1. Define the problem–for example, developing a new product or refining an old one.
2. Draw a circle and number it like a clock from 1 to 12.
3. Select any twelve attributes of the problem (e.g., of the product or service) and list these in positions 1 to 12 on the "clockface."
4. Throw a die or dice to determine the number of the first attribute to be worked on.
5. Individually or in a group, brainstorm, free associate, and/or mind map whatever thoughts about that attribute occur to you.
6. Continue rolling the dice until you have used all twelve numbers and worked on all of the attributes.
7. Make combinations of attributes, either by arbitrarily choosing combinations or by rolling the dice. Now brainstorm, free associate, and/or mind map those combinations.

35/9. COMPUTER PROGRAMS

A number of computer programs can be used to generate alternatives and otherwise add creativity to the problem-solving process. The best-known and most computationally powerful of these programs is IdeaFisher from Fisher Idea Systems. This program contains 60,000 words and phrases together with 650,000 idea-associations that are linked to several thousand questions. The questions are grouped into three divisions: (1) orientation-clarification, (2) modification, and (3) evaluation. The ques-

tions provoke ideas and associations that can be used to solve common business problems. The program has no major drawbacks.[13] Its cost is minimal.

Idea Generator Plus is another program that can be used in solving problems. It focuses mainly on walking the problem-solver through the problem solving process, making sure that all aspects of the problem have been considered. It can also be used to generate alternatives.[14]

Similarly, Ideagen walks the user through the problem solving process, but also provides random phrases to help in idea generating through free association.[15] Mindlink uses a series of mind triggers to assist problem solving. It asks the user to abandon normal association processes and go for the unusual. For example, it may ask you to link an elephant with an oil well, and then determine how this association might give clues to solving your problem. Mindlink opens with a set of creativity warm-up exercises known as The Gym. Other sections include Idea Generation, Guided Problem Solving, and General Problem Solving.[16]

Finally, The Invention Machine uses problem definition questions, a database of 1250 types of engineering problems, a database of 1230 scientific effects (e.g., physical or chemical), and examples of 2000 of the world's most innovative inventions to offer suggestions on solving your problem. Russian engineer Michael Valdman used this program to

HERMAN MILLER INNOVATES, INNOVATES, INNOVATES

Herman Miller is the second largest seller of office furniture in the U.S. It is generally regarded as the most innovative firm in the industry. It innovates in virtually every aspect of the business from products to processes of all types. It created the modular office. Ergonomic chairs and sleek looking designs are routine for the firm. Among its many other proud innovative traditions are employee participation in key decisions, and profit sharing programs for employees. Open communication and the building of a trusting work environment are other key values.

One of the most unique facets of its innovation is its efforts to be a green company (an environmentally proactive company). It has tackled its expression of concern for the environment in a responsive yet profitable way. In 1990, for example, Bill Foley, the research manager at Herman Miller, realized that the firm was using far too much wood from tropical forrests. So he sent out an edict that the firm would no longer use two species — rosewood and Honduran mahogany, once existing supplies were depleted. This threatened the sales of the firm's signature furniture product, the $2300 Eames chair which was finished in rosewood.

CONTINUES ON PAGE 74

THE INNOVATIVE EDGE IN ACTION 4.1

HERMAN MILLER

Continued from page 73

Nonetheless, the firm did exactly that, willing to suffer any reversals in sales that occured.

The firm has taken an active stance on recycling. It has reduced packaging and built an $11 million waste-to-energy heating and cooling plant that has cut its hauls to landfills by 90 percent. When Joe Azzarello, the engineer who oversees the firm's wast-to-energy plant, found out that there wasn't a good way to recycle the 800,000 styrofoam cups that employees used each year, he banned them and handed out 5,000 mugs with this Buckminster Fuller admonition: "In spaceship earth there are no passengers, only crew." The company recycles leather, vinyl, foam, office paper, phone books, and lubricating oils. Now it is trying for cradle-to-grave design that will allow recycling of all parts of its products.

The bottom line for Herman Miller is that all of these actions save it tremendous amounts of money. The waste-to-energy plant saves $750,000 a year in fuel and landfill costs. Reduced packaging saves the firm over a million dollars a year. And recycling and selling waste products saves $900,000 a year.

Source: David Woodruff, "Herman Miller: How Green is My Factory?" *Business Week,* September 16, 1991, pp. 54-56.

redesign pizza boxes. The program suggested changes in shapes and materials that led to a box that keeps pizza warm three times as long as conventional boxes.[17]

36/10. DEADLINES

Since many creative individuals work best under pressure, deadlines are extremely effective in generating alternatives and inspiring creative work. A deadline increases pressure and stimulates more right-brain activity.

37/11. DIRECT ANALOGIES

In a direct analogy facts, knowledge, or technology from one field are applied to another. Biology is a fertile field for such analogies. For example, scientists and engineers at Oregon State University have examined spiders and other bugs in an attempt to improve the agility of robots. According to one of the researchers, Eugene F. Fichter, "They're magnificent models for walking machines." Insects and spiders are filmed and their motions analyzed by computers to see whether they can be emulated by much heavier robots.[19] Similarly, scientists in England have developed new optical storage disc patterns by using the unusual eye structures of moths as an analogy. A host of products is expected to evolve from the new designs, including inexpensive medical diagnostic kits, map projection systems for automobiles, and glare-free instruments and computer screens.[20]

A few years ago a manufacturer of potato chips was faced with a frequently encountered problem: Potato chips took up too much space on the shelf when they were packed loosely, but they crumbled when they were packed in smaller packages. The manufacturer found a solution by using a direct analogy. What naturally occurring object is similar to a potato chip? How about dried leaves? Dried leaves crumble very easily, however, and are bulky. The analogy was a good one. What about pressed leaves? They're flat. Could potato chips somehow be shipped flat, or nearly flat? Unfortunately, the problem of crumbling remained. Continuing the creative process, the decision makers

realized that leaves are not pressed while they are dry but while they are moist. They determined that if they packed potato chips in a stack, moist enough not to crumble but dry enough to be flat, or nearly flat, they might just solve the problem. The result, as you may have guessed, was Pringle's.[18]

A farm products company seeking a way of planting seeds at exactly the same distance apart used a machinegun belt as an analogy. The firm created a biodegradeable tape studded with equally spaced seeds that could be laid in a furrow.[21]

When DuPont researchers were trying to develop a fire-resistant Nomex fiber that could be dyed without requiring special procedures, they were stumped because the fiber's tight structure made it impossible for dye to adhere to it. Then one of the researchers asked how miners could go into coal mines. The answer was that props keep the mine from collapsing. Applying this analogy, he embedded a large organic molecule in the fiber during manufacturing. This molecule dug a hole and propped it open so that dye could be applied. One result of this innovation is the widespread use of flame-resistant Nomex in aircraft interiors.[22]

Some direct analogies occur by chance and are followed up by creative problem solvers. At Ford Motor Company, for example, design engineers had been working unsuccessfully for months on a bucket seat that would adjust to the contours of the human body. Bill Camplisson, then director of marketing plans and programs for Ford Europe, was part of the design team. Late one night he leaned back in his seat, remembering a time he had been at the beach as a child. Someone had stepped on his beach ball and crushed it. He had begun crying and his father had come to his aid and punched out the sides of the ball. Suddenly Camplisson realized the analogy between the rubber ball and the bucket seat. The designers dropped their mechanical designs and began experimenting with new materials. Shortly thereafter they had the seat they were looking for.[23]

Think of a problem. Now write a direct analogy for that problem.

_____

_____

_____

What possible solutions emerge from your analogy?

_____

_____

A major use of analogies, and comparisons in general, is the excursion technique. This technique is usually employed after more traditional approaches, such as individual or group brainstorming, or mind mapping, have been attempted without success. Those involved put the problem aside for a while and "take an excursion" in their minds. This is essentially a word association exercise that uses visualization. A word or group of words that are colorful and have a lot of visual appeal should be used. The problem solvers spend time constructing fantasies based on the word or words chosen. Then they are asked to make a connection between their fantasies and the original problem. The "excursion" could be a trip through a natural history museum, a jungle, a zoo, or a big city. Numerous companies have used this technique successfully after other approaches have failed. The excursion technique can be used by an individual but because it is essentially a group process, it is described in Chapter 5.

SUMMARY OF STEPS

1. Find another field of science or area of endeavor that could provide an analogy to your problem.
2. Create an analogy that allows you to apply facts, knowledge, or technology from the other field to your problem
3. Determine what insights or potential solutions this analogy yields.

38/12. ESTABLISH IDEA SOURCES

To come up with ideas, I like to flip through magazines, especially *Success*, which displays lots of ideas in short boxed features. I also keep a file of over 5,000 articles and use a PC article-research data base. If you don't have places to go for ideas, find some. Take time now to make a list of possible sources of ideas. Don't limit yourself to familiar sources, search out additional places where you can get ideas. You might start with encyclopedias, science fiction books, magazines, catalogs, movies, seminars, museums, art galleries, and amusement parks, for example.

1. _____
2. _____
3. _____
4. _____
5. _____
6. _____
7. _____
8. _____
9. _____
10. _____

39/13. EXAMINE IT WITH THE SENSES

Can you use your senses (hearing, sight, touch, smell, taste) to come up with ideas about a problem, and how to solve it? List the insights and potential solutions you think of when you ask the following questions about your problem:

1. How does it feel?   _____

2. How does it smell?   _____

3. How does it look?   _____

4. What sound does it make? _____

5. What does it taste like? _____

Insights	Possible Solutions
1. _____	1. _____
2. _____	2. _____
3. _____	3. _____
4. _____	4. _____
5. _____	5. _____

Do your answers trigger any thoughts that might lead to motivations? Any solutions?

40/14. THE FCB GRID

If you are looking for new products or services to offer and are trying to figure out how to position them against those of competitors, this technique may help. The FCB grid was developed by Richard Vaughn of the advertising corporation of Foote, Cone & Belding.[24] It is a four-cell matrix similar to those commonly used to describe management and marketing concepts. Figure 4.1 portrays such a grid.

The two axes indicate positions of high and low involvement and degrees of thinking and feeling in relation to products and services. "High involvement" describes expensive products or services, such as automobiles, expensive jewelry, airplanes, and custom-designed software. "Low involvement" describes inexpensive products like dishwashing soap or fast food.

"Think" represents products or services that are evaluated according to verbal, numerical, analytical, and cognitive criteria, about which the consumer would desire more information or would have to think. Examples include computers, spreadsheet software, automobiles, and customized fitness programs. "Feel" describes products or services that appeal to the customer's emotions, about which the customer would have feelings. Examples include cosmetics, stylish clothing, and sports cars.

The axes are continuums with high and low involvement, and think and feel, at the extremes of the axes and different degrees of these variables in between. The idea is to place existing products on the grid according to their characteristics and then to find the holes in the market, that is, places where competitors don't have products.

For example, if we look at all the books on creativity techniques—and there are at least twenty such books—we find that they are, with few exceptions, low involvement/feel books. This book, *101 Creative Problem Solving Techniques*, in contrast, was designed to be a medium-involvement/think and feel book. The "think" orientation is a rational choice reflecting my perception of the market for such books. It's the "hole" in the market, or at least part of it. But, I have added some feeling characteristics in order to make the book more visual, an important aspect of increasing creativity.

The beauty of the FCB grid is that you can put anything you want on the axes. Such grids are common in marketing and strategic planning analyses. For example, Michael Porter, noted consultant, researcher, and author uses a similar grid to plot the characteristics of competitors' strategies as well as those of the subject firm. Using these strategic maps, he determines where to position the subject firm relative to other firms' strategies.[25]

You can do what Porter has done, using whatever continuums are meaningful. If, for example, you place on one axis the number of creativity techniques described in books like this one, you will find 101 techniques on one end and 10 or so on the other. This book is positioned at the "101 techniques" end of that axis. (See Figure 4.2.) On the other axis you might place the length of descriptions of techniques, with long at one end and short at the other. This book mixes the lengths, but the average is somewhere between the two extremes. As this example reveals, more than one grid may be necessary to understand the desired position of a product or service in the market.

Figure 4.1 FCB Grid

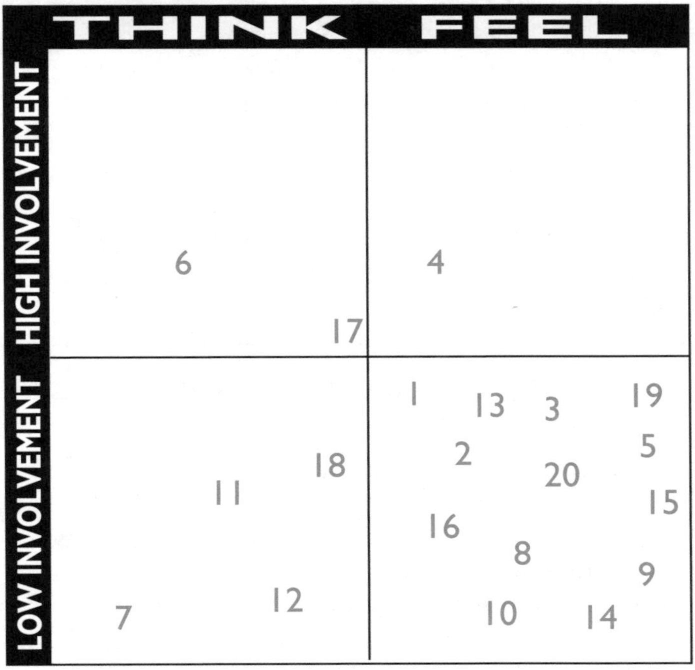

Figure 4.2 FCB Grid for Creativity Books

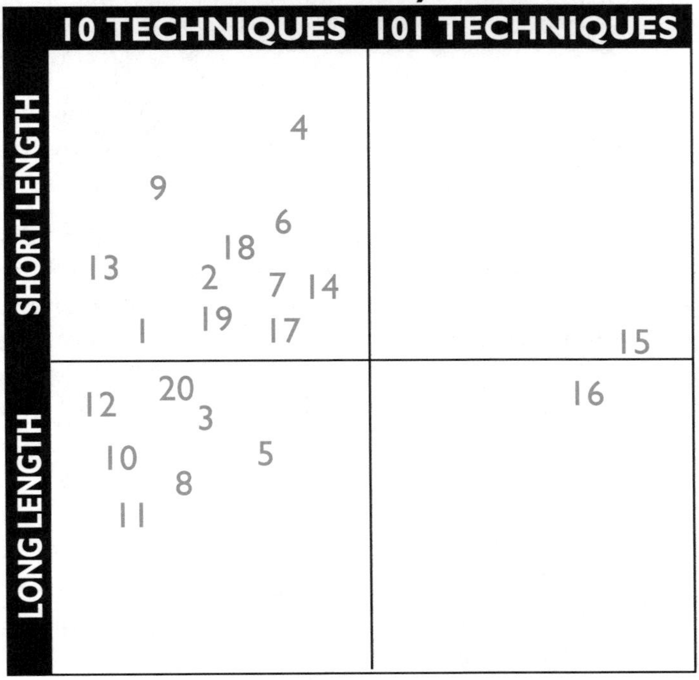

41/15. THE FOCUSED-OBJECT TECHNIQUE

The focused-object technique contains elements of both free association and forced relationships.[26] It is especially useful in situations requiring high levels of creativity, such as obtaining ideas for advertising layouts or copy. The principal difference between this technique and the other forced-relationship techniques is that one object or idea in the relationship is deliberately chosen, not selected at random.

The other object or idea is selected arbitrarily. The attributes or qualities of this second object or idea are then used as a starting point for a series of free associations. An attempt is made to adapt the resulting stream of associations to the chosen object or problem. In the case of advertising copy and art ideas, the deliberately selected object is usually the product to be advertised.

The example in Table 4.2 shows how the forced-relationship technique was used to associate with an automobile. (The automobile was the preselected object.) The attributes of the lampshade were the starting point for a chain of free associations that led to other ideas. The third column shows how the associations were applied to the problem of obtaining copy and layout ideas for the automobile.

TABLE 4.2 Application of the Focused-Object Technique

Attribute of Lampshade	Chain of Free Association	Application to Automobile
Lampshade is shaped like a peak or volcano	Volcano Volcanic power	
	Explosive power	"Engine has explosive power."
	Peak Peak of perfection	"This automobile is the peak of perfection."
	Steep hill	"It has climbing ability."
Lampshade has form	Racing form	Use a layout.
	Horses Horsepower	Show individual horse to dramatize horsepower.
	Winner's circle Fine horses	"This automobile is always in the winner's circle."
	Other fine things Morocco leather Ivory chess sets	"He likes fine cars." Associate car with fine things.
	Africa	Picture car in use in Africa and all over the world.

Source: Charles S. Whiting, "Operational Techniques of Creative Thinking," *Advanced Management*, October 1955, p. 29.

SUMMARY OF STEPS

1. Pick a product, service, or object to change.
2. List the attributes of this item.
3. Free associate words for each attribute.
4. Indicate how each free association applies to changing the item or solving the problem at hand.

42/16. FRESH EYE

Bring in someone from the outside who doesn't know anything about the problem, perhaps someone from another functional area or another company. Or bring in a consultant, someone who is an expert on creativity but not an expert in your particular field. Such a person may see the problem with a fresh eye. Not being immersed in the project, the outsider may provide some new ideas. Try getting a 6-year-old to look at the problem. Children haven't been socialized not to be creative and will say what they think; what they think might just be right.

43/17. IDEA BITS AND RACKING

Carl Gregory, author of *The Management of Intelligence*, suggests that one way of assembling "idea bits," or ideas generated in individual or group sessions, is to use a specially designed "racking board."[27] The idea slips or cards containing the ideas are placed on this racking board for examination. To construct a racking board you need some small shelf units with grooves to hold the cards. Alternatively, a magnetic device or tape can be used to stick cards to a board or wall. This technique is like storyboarding (described in Chapter 5), except that with idea bits you begin with pieces of unrelated information. Idea bits may be sudden flashes of insight, notes arising from conversations or readings, observations, objectives, information, ideas produced in a brainstorming session, new words or phrases, and so on. Putting them on a racking board allows you to look at them and see if there is any pattern to them.

44/18. IDEA NOTEBOOK

You have ideas all the time. They come to you in the shower, while sleeping, while driving. Keep a notebook or 3 x 5 cards handy to write your ideas on. You can examine them later. *Once forgotten, an idea may be lost forever. So write it down! Now!*

45/19. INPUT-OUTPUT

This technique, developed by General Electric for use in its creative engineering program, helps identify new ways to accomplish an objective, as illustrated in the following example:[28]

A dynamic system can be classified according to its (1) input, (2) output, and (3) limiting requirements or specifications. For example in designing a device to automatically shade a room during bright sunlight, the problem can be defined as follows:

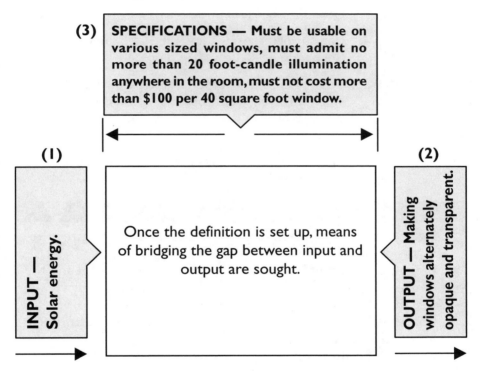

(3) SPECIFICATIONS — Must be usable on various sized windows, must admit no more than 20 foot-candle illumination anywhere in the room, must not cost more than $100 per 40 square foot window.

(1) INPUT — Solar energy.

Once the definition is set up, means of bridging the gap between input and output are sought.

(2) OUTPUT — Making windows alternately opaque and transparent.

At each step the question is asked: can this phenomenon (input) be used directly to shade the window (desired output)? Using the above example once again, we observe that solar energy is of two types, light and heat.

Step 1: What phenomena respond to application of heat? light? Are there vapors that cloud upon heating? Gases expand, metals expand, solids melt. Are there substances that cloud in bright light? Does light cause some materials to move or curl? Light causes photo-electric cells to produce current, chemicals to decompose, plants to grow.

Step 2: Can any of these phenomena be used directly to shade the window? Vapors that cloud on heating? Substances that cloud in bright light? Bi-metals warp. Slats of a blind could warp shut.

Step 3: What phenomena respond to step 1 outputs? Gases expand, could operate a bellows, etc. Photoelectric current could operate a solenoid, etc. Solids melt, effect on electric conductivity, etc.

Step 4: Can any of these phenomena be used directly to shade the window? Bellows could operate a blind, etc.

Step 5: What phenomena respond to step 3 output? Bellows, solenoid, etc., could operate a solenoid switch or valve, which in turn could operate motors to draw the blind.

In this manner a number of possible solutions can be developed for evaluation.

SUMMARY OF STEPS

1. Determine system input, desired output, and limiting requirements or specifications.
2. Brainstorm ways of bridging the gap between the input and the desired output, given the limiting requirements or specifications.
3. Use the attributes of the input to suggest solutions.
4. Continually ask the question, "Can these phenomena (attributes) lead to the desired output in any way?"
5. Evaluate the alternatives generated in this way.

46/20. LISTENING TO MUSIC

Listening to soft, calming music is a good way to "free up" your subconscious. Music is listened to on the right side of the brain, the more intuitive side (for right-handed people, the opposite for left-handed people). Music also tends to put the analytical side of the brain to sleep, allowing the intuitive side to become more active.[29]

47/21. MIND MAPPING

Mind mapping was originated by Tony Buzan of the Learning Methods Group in England.[30]   This technique is based on research findings showing that the brain works primarily with key concepts in an interrelated and integrated manner. Whereas traditional thinking opts for columns and rows, Buzan feels that "working out" from a core idea suits the brain's thinking patterns better. The brain also needs a way to "slot in" ideas that are relevant to the core idea. To achieve these ends, Buzan developed mind mapping.

Mind mapping is an individual brainstorming process. In brainstorming, you are interested in generating as many ideas as possible, even wild and crazy ones. Just write or otherwise record whatever comes into your head as it occurs. Quantity, not quality, is what you are after. No criticism is allowed during the brainstorming itself. Later you can go back and critique your inputs (or those of others in a group situation). You can also generate new ideas by looking at what you have already written—that is, "piggyback" on what has already been done. (See Chapter 5 for further discussion of this technique.)

To begin a mind mapping session, write the name or description of the object or problem in the center of a piece of paper and draw a circle around it. Then brainstorm each major facet of that object or problem, drawing lines outward from the circle like roads leaving a city. You can draw branches from those "roads" as you brainstorm them in more detail. You can brainstorm all the main lines at once and then the branches for each, or brainstorm a line and its branches, or jump from place to place as thoughts occur. To make the mind map more useful, you might draw each major branch extending from your central thought in a different color. As you branch out, you may notice related topics appearing on different branches. These relationships can be emphasized by circling the items in question, or drawing lines under or between them. Finally, study your mind map and look for interrelationships and terms appearing more than once. A sample mind map is shown in Figure 4.3. Joyce Wycoff's *Mind Mapping* [31] provides additional and very useful business examples of how to use this technique.

Figure 4.3 A Sample Mind Map

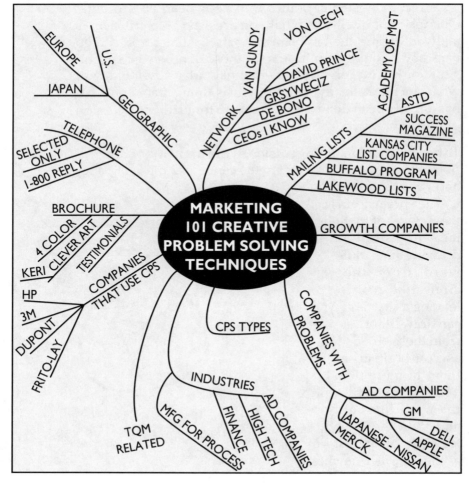

Mind mapping is an excellent technique not only for generating new ideas but also for developing one's intuitive capacity. It is especially useful for identifying all the issues and subissues related to a problem, as well as the solutions to a problem and their pros and cons. The latter is accomplished by making the main branches the solutions and the subbranches from each of these the pros and cons. Mind mapping also works well for outlining presentations, papers, and book chapters. In fact, mind mapping can be used in a wide variety of situations. For example, the extremely successful socio/technological forecasting firm, Inferential Focus, founded by Charles Hess and Carol Coleman, uses mind maps to spot trends and predict periods of change before they occur. Hess and Coleman charge a hefty $24,000 a year for their futurist publications. Their clients include the White House, Chase Manhattan Bank, First Fidelity, and numerous other Fortune 500s organizations.[32]

Numerous managers are using the mind mapping concept. For example, Michael Stanley, the engineer in charge of Boeing's technical publications unit, uses mind maps extensively. He keeps a spiral notebook of mind maps covering the "basic subjects that I've got to know to do my job." He even has a 40 foot by 4 foot mind map on his wall that he used to show top management about a new process he had designed for developing technical publications.[33] Joelle Martin, head of the agency that created Anheuser-Busch's award-winning "Being Black in America" advertising campaign, uses the technique to help her decide how and when to terminate an employee.[34]

About half of the people who learn this process find it extremely useful; the other half find it uncomfortable to use. The latter seem to object to the lack of structure and find it difficult to be as spontaneous as the process requires. But for those who are comfortable with it, it can be a very useful and versatile tool. As author Jill Neimark notes, "Once you've got the knack of letting your mind flow onto this visual chessboard (a mindmap), you can apply it to anything from business to relationships to your future."[35]

SUMMARY OF STEPS

1. Write the name or description of the object or problem in the center of a piece of paper and draw a circle around it.
2. Brainstorm each major facet of that object or problem, placing your thoughts on lines drawn outward from the central thought like roads leaving a city.
3. Add branches to the lines as necessary.
4. Use additional visual techniques–for example, different colors for major lines of thought, circles around words or thoughts that appear more than once, connecting lines between similar thoughts.
5. Study the mind map to see what interrelationships exist and what solutions are suggested.

48/22. NAME POSSIBLE USES

Naming the possible uses for an item helps provide solutions to a whole array of problems. The primary one, of course, is finding new uses for a product. Baking soda, for example, isn't just for baking. It is useable as a refrigerator deodorizer, a cleanser, and as a teeth brightener.

How many uses can you think of for a hammer? Name them.

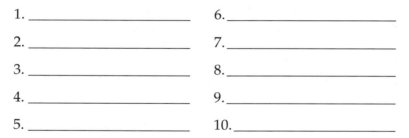

1. _____   6. _____

2. _____   7. _____

3. _____   8. _____

4. _____   9. _____

5. _____   10._____

If you want to find new uses for a product, you might be inspired by Velcro. Velcro is what you use to hold two pieces of cloth together, right? How many other uses could you think of for it? The chambers of the Jarvik-7 artifical heart are held together with Velcro for easy separation in case one side has to be replaced. Many things in the space shuttle are held together with Velcro, including parts of the rocket. Interior items, including astronauts, are held down by it. Velcro is used on blood pressure cuffs, to hold insulation in nuclear power plants, in machine gun turrets, on shoes in place of shoe strings, in automobiles to hold down batteries and spare tires, to hold together parts of an experimental car designed by Pontiac, to bind parts of airplane wings together, and to hold stamps to a letter carrier's mailbag. In fact, Velcro is a component of over 5000 patented products.[36]

Here's another example of multiple uses:

Bruce DeWoolfson reasoned that if vending machines could spit out cans and bottles for a few coins they could just as easily spit out a few coins for empty cans and bottles, which could then be recycled. His firm places these "redeemer" machines in store throughout the states where recycling is mandated by law. The firm grossed $18 million in 1986.[37]

You can use the same approach to find solutions to other problems. For instance, are you looking for a name for a product? Listing possible uses for it may suggest a good name.

49/23. THE NAPOLEON TECHNIQUE

Pretend that you are someone famous and try to solve the problem from that person's perspective.[38] Your assumed identity may give you new perspectives on a problem. For example, what would Isaac Newton do if he were confronted by your problem? General George Patton? Napoleon? Mother Theresa?

50/24. ORGANIZED RANDOM SEARCH

For many people a favorite way of coming up with new ideas is to pick a page of a dictionary at random and use the words on that page to generate ideas the way one uses a verbal checklist. You could use any book, even a catalog. Simply pick a page and look for words. Then use a two-dimensional matrix to compare the words on that page with an object or problem and/or its attributes. Sometimes you simply pick a word on that page and begin to make associations. This technique is often used by artists, writers, and others who depend on creativity for a livelihood. Managers at Current Inc., a greeting card company in Colorado Springs, picked the word "shrink." After a brainstorming session, they began Wee Greetings, a line of business and greeting cards that can be slipped into lunch boxes or shirt pockets.[39] This technique can also make use of pictures. For example, two telemarketing managers at Southern Bell leafed through fashion magazines for pictures that would trigger ideas for marketing campaigns.[40]

51/25. PERSONAL ANALOGIES

An interesting type of restrictive analogy is the "personal analogy." In this approach you attempt to see yourself personally involved in the situation, perhaps through role playing. In a 1980 personal analogy/brainstorming session at Gillette, the managers saw themselves as human hairs. They imagined how a strand of hair would observe life. "I dread being washed every day." "I hate the blow-dryer." "I feel limp, lifeless." Some participants wanted a gentle shampoo to protect their damaged ends while others wanted a more aggressive one to really get the dirt out. Sandra Lawrence, Gillette's vice-president for new products, observed that "everyone had different sentiments, which made us think about how hair is different on different parts of the body." The result was Silkience, a shampoo that adapts itself to the different needs of different kinds of hair. Within one year, Silkience was one of the top ten shampoos in total sales.[41]

A major paper company found new uses for pulp and other tree parts and significantly raised profits when top managers role played the part of a tree going through the paper production process. In another instance, scientists working to develop a reflective window glass saw themselves as the molecules of the glass. They then asked themselves, "What has to happen to us to make us reflective?" On the basis of their answers, they developed the reflective glass used in many buildings today. In a third example, state officials in Ohio who wanted to write a comprehensive computer program to keep track of automobiles saw themselves as a car and asked, "What can happen to me?"

Envision yourself as the object or other problem that you are concerned about. See how your creativity is affected. Can you put yourself into your problem? Can you be your problem? What suggestions for solutions result?

SUMMARY OF STEPS

1. Become personally involved in the problem, perhaps through role playing or visualization.
2. Ask yourself what insights or potential solutions this involvement yields.

52/26. PICTURE STIMULATION

The picture stimulation technique aims to provide ideas beyond those that might be obtained through brainstorming.[42] Picture stimulation is reminiscent of the excursion technique (see Chapter 5), except that the participants look at pictures instead of visualizing an excursion. Participants should not discuss what should or shouldn't be shown in the pictures. Discussion of the ideas suggested should not take place until the creative session is finished. Basic brainstorming rules should be followed.

1. Select pictures from various sources and present them for participants to view as transparencies or slides or in an album. The pictures should show some action and not be too abstract.
2. Examine each picture and describe it to a recorder, who writes the description on a flip chart, white board, or other surface.
3. Use each line of the description to trigger new ideas, which are recorded separately.
4. Continue until all the pictures have been examined.

53/27. PRODUCT IMPROVEMENT CHECKLIST

Arthur B. VanGundy has developed a product improvement checklist (PICL) that functions in the same way as the 36th technique discussed in this chapter—Osborn's verbal checklist. VanGundy has included some terms that seem absurd at first but that can provide new thought patterns. A total of 526 words are included in his list. Here are some examples:

Try To:	Make It:
sketch it	soft
sew it	hard
hang it	vertical
deflate it	unbreakable
gasify it	triangular
Think Of:	**Take Away or Add:**
televisions	funnels
ants	grooves
the four seasons	alcohol
bacteria	Velcro
Sir Lancelot	power

VanGundy's PICL is a recently developed process, but it is being used quite frequently. VanGundy has also developed a device that he calls the Circles of Creativity. It consists of several hundred words arranged on three concentric circles in categories such as "Try to...," "Make it...," "Think about…," "Imagine…," "Add to or delete…" Spinning the circles and using attached arrows results in several combinations of words that may suggest actions regarding an existing product or service. To receive a complete copy of PICL or the Circles of Creativity, contact Arthur B. VanGundy & Associates, 1700 Winding Ridge Road, Norman, Oklahoma 73072.

SUMMARY OF STEPS

1. Identify the product or service you wish to improve.
2. Take each of the words from the PICL and apply the verbs as directed to your product or service. Write down the results.
3. Decide which of the possible actions is most feasible.

54/28. RELATEDNESS

Coined by Donald Hambrick, the term "relatedness" refers to an exercise in which you list all businesses or products related to yours to help you think of new products for your company.[43] For example, suppose you own a radio station. Think of all the businesses even remotely related to yours: newspapers, magazines, TV, cable TV, broadcasting. Now think of businesses and products related to those: advertising, printing, publishing, satellite communication. What new products could your company generate in any of these businesses?

55/29. RELATIONAL WORDS

The verbal checklist (discussed later in this chapter) is a type of forced-relationship process. Several other such processes are worth examining; among them are the use of relational words, including verbs and prepositions; morphological analysis; and the focused-object technique. Each requires matching a set of descriptors against an object, a problem, another set of descriptors, or set of titles, such as product names.

Forced-relationship techniques can be used effectively by artists and writers and by marketers seeking to develop or name a new product. They can also be used to change something that already exists or when one is seeking a new and different idea rather than a solution to a specific problem. These techniques are not well suited to solving specific problems because they rely primarily on chance relationships, and the probability of such a relationship existing as a specific problem is remote. However, if your problem is to add creativity to an existing situation, these processes are excellent. Techniques 55/29 and 56/30 are forced-relationship techniques. Technique 56/30 is also partly a form of free association.

Several relational word checklists exist. Three of them are provided on the following pages. The verbs would be used in the same way as Osborn's verbal checklist, technique 62/36. With the relational words and prepositions, you are simply trying to create ideas that might lead to product or service improvements. Some of your results might seem not to make sense, but by looking at them closely you may be able to develop useful ideas.

SUMMARY OF STEPS

1. Identify the product or service to be altered, or the object to be changed.
2. Apply the words from the various checklists to this product, service or object, recording the results in the spaces provided on the forms.
3. Review the results to see if they suggest possible solutions.

A Verbal Relational-Word Checklist[44]

Multiply _____

Divide _____

Eliminate _____

Subdue _____

Invert _____

Separate _____

Transpose _____

Unify _____

Dissect _____

Distort _____

Rotate _____

Flatten _____

Squeeze _____

Complement _____

Submerge _____

Freeze _____

Soften _____

Fluff Up _____

By-Pass _____

Add _____

Subtract _____

Widen _____

Repeat _____

Thicken _____

Stretch _____

Extrude _____

Help _____

Protect _____

Segregate _____

Integrate _____

Symbolize _____

Abstract _____

Etc. _____

Crovitz's Relational Words[45]

The words in this list are used to ask questions: What's about this problem? What's across from this problem? What comes after this problem? And so on. The purpose is to generate ideas. Once you have ideas, analyze them to see what solutions they suggest.

About _____

Across _____

After _____

Against _____

Among _____

And _____

As _____

At _____

Because _____

Before _____

Between _____

But _____

By _____

Down _____

For _____

From _____

If _____

In _____

Near _____

Not _____

Now _____

Of _____

Off _____

Opposite _____

Or _____

Out _____

Over _____

Around _____

Still _____

So _____

Then _____

Though _____

Through _____

Till _____

To _____

Under _____

Up _____

When _____

Where _____

While _____

With _____

VanGundy's Prepositions[46]

These words can be used in the same way as Crovitz's relational words.

Above _____

Along _____

Amid _____

Around _____

Behind _____

Below _____

Beneath _____

Beside _____

Beyond _____

During _____

Except _____

Into _____

Past _____

Since _____

Toward _____

Throughout _____

Upon _____

Within _____

Without _____

56/30. REVERSAL-DEREVERSAL

The reversal-dereversal technique can provide insights into new solutions for a problem.[47] State the problem, using an action verb. Then take the antonym of that verb and solve the new problem created in this way. The solutions to that problem may give you ideas about solving the original problem. For example, "to improve the product" would reversal-dereversal as "to worsen" the product. If the product was a stereo, you could cut out the sound; make the speakers smaller; make it have one medium only—record, cassette, or CD; or you could reduce sound quality. The opposites of these would normally help solve the original problem. But also, making the speakers smaller could actually lead to a better product if the sound quality could be maintained. Maybe a new type of speaker is needed.

100

57/31. ROLLING IN THE GRASS OF IDEAS

This technique involves collecting as much material as you can about the problem at hand in an easily readable form— for example, summaries of related articles and books, the experiences of others, ideas that others have given you, and competitors' actions. You read through this material as rapidly as you can in one sitting. Then you ask yourself what it all means. Are there any patterns? If so, what do they suggest? What solutions pop into your head?

This technique is especially useful for solving management or technical problems, writing talks, articles or papers, or book chapters, and creating models of situations. It is the volume of ideas that can be associated with each other that makes this technique work.

The name of this technique came from watching my two Irish setters, Misty and Macintosh. We've all seen dogs roll on their backs in the grass. Misty and Macintosh would also roll on their backs in notes, articles, or manuscript pages lying on the floor of my office. One day I told students in my innovation class how I sometimes get ideas for articles, books, products, management problems, and other problems by reading through as much material as possible related to the problem at hand. I described how excited I get with all those ideas running through my head, and how insights seem to pop into my head as a result. The analogy to my dogs' behavior was a natural: I am rolling in the grass of ideas.

SUMMARY OF STEPS

1. Collect information about your problem, making notes in an easily readable form.
2. Read through all of your notes in one sitting so that all the ideas are in your brain at one time.
3. Allow natural incubation to occur and see what ideas develop.

58/32. THE 7 x 7 TECHNIQUE

Another way to improve the utilization of new ideas is the 7 x 7 technique, a series of exercises designed to process, organize and evaluate idea slips that have been mounted on a racking board in seven rows and seven columns (or more, if needed).[48] Carl Gregory, who developed this technique, suggests that the following steps can help you make sense of all your ideas. You might use suggestions for this technique with a similar process, storyboarding (see Chapter 5):

1. Combine similar ideas.
2. Exclude irrelevant data.
3. Modify ideas to reflect insights gained in the first two steps.
4. Defer extraneous data for future reference.
5. Review past exercises to identify possibilities for alteration or refinement.
6. Classify dissimilar groupings into separate columns.
7. Rank items in each column.
8. Generalize each column using its main idea as a heading or title.
9. Rank the columns from left to right on the racking board according to their importance or utility.

Brief explanations of these steps follow.

Combine

When you have at least two racking boards filled with idea slips or when your pile of ideas is exhausted, read each idea bit carefully. Discard any redundant information and combine similar ideas. Give each grouping of related ideas a title.

Exclude

Exclude all things that are not related to the objective of the exercise or are too "far out" for present consideration. Put the excluded ideas into another pile for later use.

Modify

Where necessary, write new statements of ideas that have been modified as a result of the first two steps.

Defer

Put into a separate category any item that is not particularly timely but may be useful later. Defer is similar to exclude except the criteria are different.

Feedback

Review the ideas that have been combined, eliminated, modified, or deferred to seek new insights.

Classify by Dissimilar Columns

Establish a column for each group of related ideas. Despite the name of the technique, seven is not a magic number: eight, nine, ten, or more columns may be necessary.

Rank Ideas in Each Column

When you have sorted all the ideas into columns, rank each idea card on the basis of the usefulness or importance of the idea relative to the objective.

Generalize Columns

It is often advantageous to provide a title for each column, as in storyboarding. You could probably put those which are similar under the same column heading. Alternatively, the highest-ranking idea in each column could serve as the heading.

Rank Columns

Place the best, most important, timeliest, or most critical ideas in the left-hand column, the second-most important in the next column to the right, and so on.

There are many variations on the 7 x 7 technique. Like storyboarding, it can be used in group sessions.

SUMMARY OF STEPS

1. Place idea slips on a 7 x 7 racking board.
2. Combine, exclude, modify, defer, feedback, classify, and rank ideas within columns; generalize the columns; and then rank the columns.
3. Evaluate the results.

59/33. SLEEPING/DREAMING ON IT

One of the easiest ways to generate alternatives is to think rationally, very hard, and very long about a problem just before going to sleep. Put it out of your mind and then go to sleep. When you wake up in the morning, the odds are that you will have come up with an interesting alternative or series of alternatives for solving the problem. The reason this technique works so well is that your subconscious continues to work on the problem while you are asleep.

Thomas Edison often used brief periods of sleep to develop ideas. He would sit in a chair and holding pebbles in his hands allow himself to fall asleep while thinking about a problem. As he fell asleep, the pebbles would fall from his hands into tin plates on the floor. This, he claimed, helped him come up with new ideas by taking advantage of his subconscious efforts to solve problems in a state of near-sleep.[49]

Solutions to complex problems often appear in dreams. The concept of the benzene molecule came to German chemist Friedrick August Kelkule in a dream. He saw a snake biting its own tail and realized that the benzene molecule was a closed loop, not an open one. Noted writer Robert Louis Stevenson, who often used his subconscious to develop story ideas, reports that the characters of Dr. Jekyll and Mr. Hyde came to him in a dream.[50]

SUMMARY OF STEPS

1. Think long and hard about your problem just before going to sleep and as you begin to drift off.
2. If you awake during the night with a solution or other ideas, write them down on notecards that you have left on the nightstand next to your bed.
3. When you awake in the morning, think about your thoughts and dreams and see if they suggest solutions to your problem. Write the possible solutions on notecards.

60/34. THE TWO-WORDS TECHNIQUE

The meaning you give to certain words can block your ability to solve a problem. With the two-words technique you pick the two words or phrases from your problem statement that indicate its essence. The problem statement always includes a subject (or objective) and an action verb. Normally you focus on these in the two-words technique.[51]

For example, suppose that the problem statement is "Reduce absenteeism." You have been unable to generate many new ideas about how to solve the problem. You might list the following alternate words:

reduce	absenteeism
diminish	out
decrease	away
shorten	not in
curtail	not present
lessen	lacking
contract	missing

Then you might try combining these words in various ways. The following ideas could result:

1. Design an absenteeism program in which employees are given a certain number of days per year for "no excuse needed" absences (diminish/not in).

2. Survey employees to find what might be lacking in the workplace to cause them to be absent (decrease/lacking).

3. Lower the penalty for unauthorized absences if the absence was for less than a day (shorten/out).

4. Allow employees to be absent a specified number of days during a given quarter if they make up for them during the next quarter (curtail/away).

5. Offer employees the opportunity to benefit from self- or professional-development programs on the job. This might increase their motivation and decrease the number of absences (less/lacking)."

101
CREATIVE
PROBLEM
SOLVING
TECHNIQUES

105

This is an excellent technique for overcoming definitional problems, but it can also be used to generate new ideas even if you aren't having problems with the definitions of terms.

SUMMARY OF STEPS

1. Select two key words or phrases (usually the action verb and the objective) from the problem statement.
2. List alternate words for each word or phrase (a thesaurus or dictionary may be helpful).
3. Select the first word from the first list and combine it with the first word from the second list.
4. Examine this combination and see if it suggests any ideas. If so, write them down.
5. Combine the first word from the first list with the second word from the second list.
6. Continue combining words from the two lists and writing down ideas until you have examined all possible combinations.

61/35. USING THE COMPUTER TO STIMULATE CREATIVITY

Computers like the Producer ($5000 to $9000) allow special effects to be built into presentations, for example, a pie chart may appear in 3-D and be rotated as it moves through space. Software packages such as "Mac Paint," and "PC Paintbrush" allow the user to construct art-based presentations. Software packages such as Freehand, Designer, CorelDraw, Artline, and Powerpoint allow for exciting graphic art and word presentations. "Deluxe Video Software" allows you to combine materials from a VCR with a PC presentation. Exciting graphics and overlaid background scenes are frequently employed. Computer aided design (CAD) uses highly sophisticated computers and software to aid in product design. A number of additional programs enable you to change artwork on a PC far more quickly than by hand.[52]

62/36. VERBAL CHECKLIST FOR CREATIVITY

A checklist of questions about an existing product, service, process, or other item under consideration can yield new points of view and thereby lead to innovation. The most

frequently
used creative alterna-
tive generation check-
list, the verbal checklist, was developed by Alex Osborn while
he was a partner of a major U. S. advertising firm. Osborn
also originated the most frequently used group process for
generating alternatives, brainstorming, which will be described in Chapter 5. These two processes were first described to the general public in 1953.[53] Only a few of the
techniques developed since that time have proven to be as
effective as Osborn's two major contributions.

The idea behind the verbal checklist is that an existing product or service, whether one's own or a competitor's, can be
improved if one applies a series of questions to it and pur-
sues the answers to see where they may lead. The main questions take the form of verbs such as <u>Modify?</u> or <u>Combine?</u>
These verbs indicate possible ways to improve an existing
product or service by making changes in it. In the case of
Osborn's checklist, further alternatives may be suggested by
the definitions and related statements accompanying each
of the main verbs. For example, if the item under consideration is a laptop PC and you are pursuing the "minify" alternative, you might shrink the laptop into a "notebook" or
"palmtop" computer.

Over the years thousands of organizations have used the verbal checklist to create or enhance thousands of products and services. I have utilized it myself in writing some of the most successful books in the college textbook market, including *The Management Challenge*, an introductory management text.[54] One of my editors has found the checklist so useful that he distributed it to the sales force to obtain suggestions for subsequent editions.

Table 4.3 presents the Osborn verbal checklist. On the next page is a form for you to complete, either as practice in using the process or as an actual exercise in product/service improvement. You may wish to add other verbs to the list. Some of the verbs in the checklist do not apply as readily to services as they do to products, but each of them should be considered. Be sure to use the expanded definitions of these verbs as guides in changing the product or service in question. If you feel especially creative, you can make up your own checklist—for example, one designed strictly for services.

TABLE 4.3 The Osborn Verbal Checklist

Put to Other Uses?	New ways to use as is? Other uses if modified?
Adapt?	What else is like this? What other idea does this suggest? Does past offer parallel? What could I copy? Whom could I emulate?
Modify?	New twist? Change meaning, color, motion, sound, odor, form, shape? Other changes?
Magnify?	What to add? More time? Greater frequency? Stronger? Higher? Longer? Thicker? Extra value? Plus ingredient? Duplicate? Multiply? Exaggerate?
Minify?	What to subtract? Smaller? Condensed? Miniature? Lower? Shorter? Lighter? Omit? Streamline? Split up? Understate?
Substitute?	Who else instead? What else instead? Other ingredient? Other material? Other process? Other power? Other place? Other approach? Other tone of voice?
Rearrange?	Interchange components? Other pattern? Other layout? Other sequence? Transpose cause and effect? Change pace? Change schedule?
Reverse?	Transpose positive and negative? How about opposites? Turn it backward? Turn it upside down? Reverse role? Change shoes? Turn tables? Turn other cheek?
Combine?	How about a blend, an alloy, an assortment, an ensemble? Combine units? Combine purposes? Combine appeals? Combine ideas?

Source: Alex Osborn, *Applied Imagination*, (New York: Charles Scribner's & Sons, 1953), p. 284.
Reprinted with the permission of The Creative Edge Foundation, Buffalo, New York.

TABLE 4.4 Osborn Checklist Completion Form

ITEM _____

Put to other uses _____

Adapt _____

Modify _____

Magnify _____

Minify _____

Substitute _____

Rearrange _____

Reverse _____

Combine _____

To use this checklist to generate new ideas, enter the name of the product or service in the blank at the top of the page (Table 4.4). Then apply the verbs and definitions from the Osborn Checklist to that item, recording your new ideas in the blanks by the verbs. A typical checklist session might last from fifteen minutes to an hour or more. In a group members can compare their answers and build on each other's suggestions.

SUMMARY OF STEPS

1. Identify the product or service to be modified.
2. Apply each of the verbs on the checklist to suggest changes in the product or service, writing the changes in the blank spaces on the form provided.
3. Make sure you use each of the definitional words for the listed verbs in identifying possible changes.
4. Review your changes to determine which ones meet your solution criteria.

101
CREATIVE
PROBLEM
SOLVING
TECHNIQUES

109

63/37. VISUALIZATION

Visualization of a problem and its potential solutions is a good way to generate alternatives. The mind seems to react even more creatively to pictures than to words. Visualization seems to evoke new insights, which can lead to new solutions. This process can be used in conjunction with other processes.[55] Simply close your eyes and visualize the problem. What do you see? Expand on what you see. Seek more detail. What do your visions suggest? What solutions can you see?

64/38 WHAT IF...?

Ask yourself "What if something happens, what would the consequences be?" For example, what if you sold a million units of your product next year? What consequences would occur? Who would be affected? What actions should you take? Or if your sales dropped by 10 percent, how would your firm be affected? What should you do?

This technique can be a powerful tool. Successful strategic management often depends on the ability to use software to ask "What if" questions and then generate a list of consequences and strategic responses. Firms often use "What if" scenarios to formulate strategic plans and strategic contingency plans. About 80 percent of astronaut training is responding to "What if" situations.[56]

A FINAL NOTE

There are thirty-eight processes discussed in this chapter. Some you will like, some you won't, but try as many of them as you can. Then use the ones you feel most comfortable with, but revisit the rest of these processes occasionally to make sure you aren't overlooking one that might be of value in your particular situation. Table 4.5 contains a quick guide to my favorite individual and group alternative generation techniques.

CHRYSLER REINVENTS AUTOMOBILE DESIGN

Reeling from foreign competition and the inability to get new products to market quickly enough, Chrysler Corporation decided that it had to reinvent its product design operation. It developed the $1 billion Chrysler Technical Center (CTC). To speed product development at the CTC, Chrysler created four cross functional platform teams to develop new products: large car, small car, minivan and jeep/truck. Representatives of each of the functional departments, plus customers, were integrated into the product development, manufacturing and marketing processes. Finance was integrated into the loop, but the team was charged with bringing the new model in within precise budgets. Each team has its own floor in the CTC.

The CTC includes a manufacturing facility where prototype manufacturing processes can be developed at the same time that a new car is being designed in order to speed manufacturing and improve quality. The platform team works in conjunction with assembly line workers to determine the best manufacturing processes and procedures for the new models. This process innovation is unique in the automobile industry.

Accompanying Chrysler's changes in product development have been changes in management style, organizational structure, and organizational culture. In concert, employees have been empowered, the organization decentralized and a competitive culture infused throughout the firm.

The results have been impressive. Chrysler's Viper sports car was an instant success, as have been its new LH cars which include the Dodge Intrepid, Eagle Vision, and the Chrysler Concorde, New Yorker, and LHS models. Chrysler's stock has soared from a low of $10.50 in 1991 to a high of $57 in the fall of 1993.

Sources: Brian S. Moskal, "Chrysler Polishes the Creative Wheel," *Industry Week*, March 16, 1992, pp. 40-42; and Peter M. Tobias and Shari Johnson, "Chrysler Harnesses Brainpower," *Industry Week*, September 21, 1992, pp. 16-20.

THE INNOVATIVE EDGE IN ACTION 4.2

TABLE 4.5

A QUICK GUIDE TO MY FAVORITE TECHNIQUES FOR GENERATING ALTERNATIVES*

INDIVIDUAL TECHNIQUES

Technique	Best Use
Verbal Checklist/Product Improvement Checklist	For redesigning existing products and services
Mind Mapping	To let ideas flow freely; for designing outlines; for collecting thoughts about an issue
Association/ Free Association	When you need lots of ideas quickly and a way to relate them to problems; when normal processes haven't provided many ideas
Rolling in the Grass of Ideas	For gaining new insights, combining ideas, and solving complex problems about which much is known

GROUP TECHNIQUES**

Technique	Best Use
Brainstorming	For simple problems when solutions are needed quickly
Lotus Blossom	To generate lots of ideas quickly to size up a problem; excellent for developing future scenarios
Storyboarding	For understanding issues involved in complex problems, and for solving complex problems
Excursion	When problem is difficult to solve, when it has been hard to generate ideas using other techniques
Nominal Group Technique	Especially useful when you want to keep one person from dominating the choice among alternatives
Morphological Analysis	For generating lots of ideas quickly about product or service improvements

**All except the nominal group technique can be used individually as well as in a group.

*For another author's view of her favorite seven techniques see Joyce Wycoff, *Transformation Thinking: Tools and Techniques That Make Every Member of Your Company a Great Thinker* (Berkely, CA: Berkely Publishing Group, 1994).

REFERENCES

[1] Marc Hequet, "Creativity Training Gets Creative," *Training* (February 1992), pp. 41–45; Charlene Marmer Soloman, "Creativity Training: What An Idea," *Personnel Journal* (May 1990), pp. 64–71; Bennett Davis, "Working the Imagination," *USAIR,* (September 1988), pp. 18-27.

[2] Peter Rodelsky, "The Man Who Mastered Motion," *Science* (May 1986), pp. 53, 54.

[3] Magaly Olivero, "Get Crazy! How to Have a Breakthrough Idea," *Working Woman* (September 1990), p. 198.

[4] Robert W. Boozer, David C. Wyld, and James Grant, "Using Metaphor to Create More Effective Sales Messages," *Journal of Services Marketing* (Summer 1990), pp. 63-71.

[5] Ikujiro Nonaka, "The Knowledge-Creating Company," *Harvard Business Review* (November-December 1991), p. 100.

[6] Source unknown.

[7] Mark Golin, "How to Brainstorm by Yourself ... and Triple the Results," *Young Executive* (Spring 1992), p. 75.

[8] Bryan W. Mattimore, "Breakthroughs: Creatively Destroying the Barriers to Business Innovation," *Success* (November 1988), p. 46.

[9] Arthur B. VanGundy, *Creative Problem Solving* (New York: Quorum Books, 1987), pp. 123-124.

[10] Charles S. Whiting, "Operational Techniques of Creative Thinking," *Advanced Management* (October 1955), p. 26.

[11] Dan Koberg and Jim Bagnall, *Universal Traveler* (Los Altos, CA: William Kaufman, Inc., 1974), p. 50.

[12] Michael Michalko, *Thinkertoys: A Handbook of Business Creativity for the 1990s,* (Berkeley, CA: Ten Speed Press, 1991), pp. 181-185.

[13] Joseph M. Winski, "Big Idea in Box," *Advertising Age* (March 25, 1991), pp. 31; E. W. Brody, "Software Reviews: IdeaFisher 3.0," *Public Relations Review,* (Winter 1990), pp. 67-68.

[14] Winski, op. cit.; Bryan W. Mattimore, "Mind Blasters: Software to Shatter Brain Block," *Success* (June 1990), pp. 46, 47.

[15] Jenny C. McCune, "Creativity Catalysts," *Success* (July/August 1992), p. 50.

[16] Ibid.

[17] Bryan Mattimore, "The Amazing Invention Machine," *Success* (October 1993), p. 34.

[18] Berkeley Rice, "Imagination to Go," *Psychology Today* (May 1984), p. 48.

[19] "Want to Design a Robot? Try Watching a Bug," *Business Week* (1986), pp. .

[20] G. Berton Latamore, "Moth's Eyes Inspire Advances in Optical Changes," *High Technology* (April 1987), p. 67.

[21] Magaly Olivero, op. cit., p. 148.

[22] James Braham, "Creativity: Eureka!" *Machine Design* (February 6, 1992), p. 37.

[23] Michael Ray and Rochelle Myers, *Creativity in Business,* (New York, Doubleday, 1986), p. 6.

[24] Michalko, op. cit., pp. 126-131.

[25] Michael E. Porter, *Competitive Advantage* (New York: Free Press, 1985), pp. 131-151.

[26] Charles S. Whiting, op. cit., p. 29.

[27] Carl E. Gregory, *The Management of Intelligence* (New York: McGraw-Hill, 1962), pp. 45-51.

[28] Dan Koberg and Jim Bagnall, op. cit., p. 27.

101
CREATIVE
PROBLEM
SOLVING
TECHNIQUES

113
n

[29] Anne H. Rosenfeld, "Music, The Beautiful Disturber," *Psychology Today* (December 1985), pp. 48–56; 71.

[30] Tony Buzan, *Use Both Sides of Your Brain*, (New York: E.P. Dutton, Inc., 1983).

[31] Joyce Wycoff, *Mind Mapping*, (Berkley Publishing Group: 1991).

[32] Jill Neimark, "Mind Mapping," *Success* (June 1986), pp. 52–57.

[33] James Braham, op. cit., p. 33.

[34] Jill Neimark, op. cit., p. 54.

[35] Ibid.

[36] Judith Stone, "Velcro: The Final Frontier," *Discover* (May 1988), pp. 82-84.

[37] "Inside Track: Finding Riches in Garbage," *Success* (May 1987), p. 30.

[38] Bryan W. Mattimore, "Breakthroughs: Creatively Destroying the Barriers to Business Innovation," *Success* (November 1988), p. 48.

[39] Emily T. Smith, "Are You Creative?" *Business Week* (September 30, 1985), p. 48.

[40] Author's conversation with these two attendees at one of my seminars.

[41] Magaly Olivero, op. cit., p. 145.

[42] Arthur B. VanGundy, *Creative Problem Solving*, op. cit., pp. 136-137.

[43] "Buzzword of the Month," *Success* (November 1985), p. 20.

[44] Source unknown.

[45] H.F. Crovitz, *Galton's Walk* (New York: Harper & Row, 1970).

[46] Arthur B. VanGundy, *Techniques of Structured Problem Solving* (New York: Van Norstrand Reinhold, 1988), p. 105.

[47] Edward Glassman, "Creative Problem Solving," *Supervisory Management* (March 1989), pp. 14-18.

[48] Carl E. Gregory, op. cit., pp. 45-51.

[49] From a lecture given in the guided tour of Edison's winter home in Ft. Myers, Florida, May 17, 1987.

[50] Robert Wayne Johnston, "Using Dreams for Creative Problem Solving," *Personnel* (November 1987), pp. 58–63; Edward Ziegler, "Dreams: The Genie Within," *Reader's Digest* (September 1985), pp. 77–81.

[51] Arthur B. VanGundy, *Creative Problem Solving*, op. cit., pp. 118-120.

[52] Christine Castro, "Drawing and Illustration Software: New Tools of the Artist's Trade: Buyer's Guide to Drawing and Illustration Programs," *Computer Publishing Magazine* (February 1991), pp. 32-46; "This Computer Unleashes the Walt Disney in You," *Business Week* (October 26, 1987), p. 119; Mark Lewyn, "VCR Plus PC Equals Effects," *USA Today* (February 17, 1988), p. 10B; Michell Rogers, "Creative Computers," *Newsweek* (April 25, 1988), pp. 54-55.

[53] Alex F. Osborn, *Applied Imagination*, (New York: Charles Scribner's & Sons, 1953).

[54] James M. Higgins, *The Management Challenge*, 2nd ed., (New York: MacMillan, 1994).

[55] Lea Hall, "Can You Picture That?" *Training & Development Journal* (September 1990), pp. 79-81.

[56] Edgar Mitchell (former astronaut) cited in Roy Rowan, *The Intuitive Manager* (Boston: Little, Brown, 1986), p. 13.

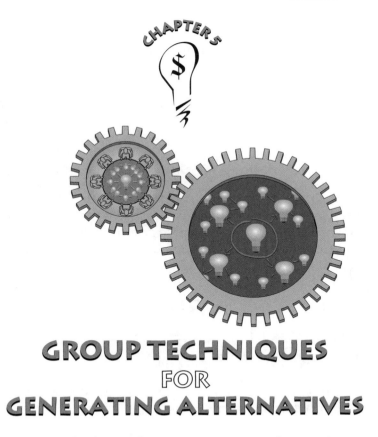

Advantages
and
Disadvantages
of Group
Decision
Making

•

Group
Processes for
Generating
Creative
Alternatives

GROUP TECHNIQUES
FOR
GENERATING ALTERNATIVES

Innovating ... has become the most urgent concern of corporations everywhere.

— Kenneth Labich
Author, *Fortune*

Since much work is performed in groups, many of the approaches to management that are currently favored focus on work groups such as autonomous work teams and self-management programs.[0] Moreover, in recent years groups have been the focus of attempts to improve quality and productivity, for example through quality circles. As research and experience indicate that groups usually provide better solutions than individuals, it makes sense to focus on group-based techniques for generating creative alternatives. And if you, as a manager or small-group leader, want your group to be more effective, you will want to train the members of your group in the processes that make groups more successful in generating creative alternatives.

101
CREATIVE
PROBLEM
SOLVING
TECHNIQUES

115

This chapter first discusses the advantages and disadvantages of group decision making and then reviews in some detail the major group-based techniques for generating alternatives: brainstorming, creativity circles, the excursion technique, group decision support systems (including electronic brainstorming), lotus blossom, morphological analysis, the nominal-group technique, storyboarding, and synectics. Several other group processes are discussed briefly.

For our purposes there are two types of groups: interactive and noninteractive. In interactive groups the participants meet face to face; in noninteractive groups they do not meet. Except for the Delphi technique, the processes discussed in this chapter involve interactive groups.

ADVANTAGES AND DISADVANTAGES OF GROUP DECISION MAKING

Groups offer six advantages over individual decision making and problem solving:[1]

1. The group can provide a better solution to that of an individual. Collectively the members of a group have more knowledge than an individual. Interactive groups not only combine this knowledge but create a knowledge base greater than the sum of its parts as individuals build on each other's inputs.

2. Those who will be affected by a decision or must implement it accept it more readily if they have a say in making it.

3. Group participation leads to a better understanding of the decision.

4. Groups help ensure a broader search effort.

5. The propensity to take risks is balanced. Individuals who are highly likely to take risks often fail. Groups moderate this tendency. Conversely, groups encourage the risk avoider to take more risks.

6. There is usually a better collective judgment.

On the other hand, there are some liabilities to employing group decision making and problem solving:[2]

1. In interactive groups there is pressure to conform. Sometimes these groups become susceptible to what is known as "group think," in which people begin to think alike and not tolerate new ideas or ideas contrary to those of the group.

2. One individual may dominate the interactive group so that his or her opinions prevail over those of the group. Nominal groups are designed to overcome this problem.

3. Groups typically require more time to come to decisions than individuals do.

4. Although groups usually make better decisions than the average individual, they seldom make better ones than the superior individual. In fact, superior performance by a group may result from the efforts of one superior group member.

5. Spending an excessive amount of time arriving at a consensus may negate the advantages of a good decision.

6. Groups sometimes make riskier decisions than they should. This propensity of groups is known as the risky shift.

When you weigh the pros and cons, the advantages win out. But when using groups to generate creative solutions don't forget their limitations.

101
CREATIVE
PROBLEM
SOLVING
TECHNIQUES

117

GROUP PROCESSES FOR GENERATING CREATIVE ALTERNATIVES

The remainder of this chapter examines the various group processes for generating alternatives. Don't overlook any of them, since they may all help you in one way or another. I try to use them all occasionally, although, my favorites are these four:

65/1.	Brainstorming
74/10.	Excursion technique
83/19.	Lotus blossom
93/29.	Storyboarding

See Table 4.5, page 112, for a quick guide to these processes.

65/1. BRAINSTORMING

Brainstorming is one of the most effective, and probably the most widely used, of the group processes.[3] It was created over sixty years ago by Alex Osborn of the advertising firm of Batten, Barton, Durstine and Osborn to increase the quantity and quality of advertising ideas.[4] The process became known as brainstorming because the participants' brains were used to "storm" a problem. Alternative solutions are offered verbally by group members in spontaneous fashion as they think of them. The leader acknowledges each contribution, which is recorded on a board for all to see. Wild and crazy ideas are encouraged. Quantity, not quality, counts at first. In the initial session there is no discussion or criticism. The ideas are evaluated at later meetings of the same group.

The Group: The brainstorming process involves a group of six to twelve people, a leader/facilitator and a secretary, all involved in open generation of ideas about a given topic. The group needs to have at least six people in order to generate enough ideas, but fewer than thirteen because it may be difficult to absorb a large number of ideas and because larger groups tend to intimidate some people, thereby potentially restricting the flow of ideas. Groups may be formed from similar or different work areas or backgrounds, depending on the purpose of the group.

The Rules:

1. No judgments are made about any suggestion.

2. All ideas, even absurd or impractical ones, are welcome.

3. Quantity of ideas is a major objective, since it leads to quality.

4. Ideas may be combined, refined, and piggy-backed.

101
CREATIVE
PROBLEM
SOLVING
TECHNIQUES

119

The Role of the Group Leader: The group leader, usually chosen prior to the session, informs the group, preferably in advance of their meeting, that a given topic will be discussed. He or she sets forth the facts, the issues, the questions involved, and the purposes of the session. These points should be restated at the beginning of the session. The leader then writes the focal question or problem on a whiteboard or other large visible surface. (Open-ended "how" or "what" questions are advisable.) Next the leader calls for solutions to the problem. Once the brainstorming session opens, the leader functions primarily as a facilitator, recognizing contributors, stimulating group members to come up with new ideas, keeping the group focused on the subject at hand, and making sure the four rules of brainstorming are followed. The most important of these rules is that no criticism is allowed. *If criticism occurs while ideas are being generated, the whole point of brainstorming has been lost.* The leader too must refrain from commenting on the value of ideas.

Sometimes group members begin to tire and the flow of new ideas diminishes. At this time the leader should offer verbal encouragement or call on particular members to suggest solutions. Another method is to give each member thirty seconds to come up with a new idea, moving around the room in order until the time allotted for the session is gone.

The same leader or a different one may lead the evaluation session. Ideas should be sorted into types and ranked according to priority. As additional research may be necessary, the group may have to convene more than once. In an evaluation session the leader must not allow the group to dismiss ideas simply because they are unusual, but should encourage examination of far-out suggestions, perhaps by asking for different versions or ways to adapt them. Moreover, the leader should not allow ideas to be dismissed because of a lack of funds or other resources. If an idea is a good one, ways should be found to make it happen. The leader's role includes counteracting unreasonable negativity during the evaluation process.

The Secretary: The secretary records each contributor's ideas on some visible surface in front of the group. In small groups the leader and the secretary may be the same person, but it is preferable to have different people performing these functions.

Observations on the Technique

Research has found that brainstorming generates a much greater number of ideas than normal group problem solving. Its features of spontaneity, suspended judgment, and absence of criticism promote an increase not only in the quantity but also in the quality of new ideas. A typical idea generation session, being very intensive, should last no more than thirty to forty minutes. Problem topics should be narrow, and no more than one topic should be covered in a session. For example, don't try to name a product and figure out a distribution system in thirty minutes.

Because the process appears simple, you may be tempted to discount this method. Don't. Thousands of organizations have used brainstorming successfully. I can personally attest to its worth, but must confess that I was a "doubting Thomas" until I used it. You cannot imagine the synergism resulting from this method unless you try it.

Brainstorming can be used for a wide diversity of problems, including not only marketing and product issues but strategy, planning, policy, organization, leadership, staffing, motivation, control, and communication. However, the process is not particularly useful with broad and complex problems. Some of the ideas produced may be of low quality or obvious generalities. Brainstorming is not successful in situations that require trial and error as opposed to judgment. There are no apparent rewards for group members other than the experience of participation and ownership. Group members may not see the final solution implemented and may therefore be reluctant to participate in further sessions.[5] Nevertheless, brainstorming remains a solid technique for generating creative ideas.

Experiences with the Process

Many organizations use brainstorming to solve a wide variety of problems. For example, International Paper Company (IP) has opened a Packaging Innovation Center in Middletown, New York, to help its customers design the best possible packages for their products. The IP center brings customers together with IP's package designers, scientists,

101
CREATIVE
PROBLEM
SOLVING
TECHNIQUES

121

technicians and product specialists for brainstorming sessions. In the first few months of operations the Innovation Center's efforts resulted in four new, economically significant, innovative package designs:[6]

1. Box & box—intended to replace plastic pails and metal containers,

2. Xpack—a flat-topped liquid container with superior shipping characteristics,

3. Barrier plus—a series of linerless folding cartons with a variety of closures and designs,

4. A new kraft paper that decomposes 50 percent faster than previously used papers.

At DuPont Imaging Systems and Electronics division, technical staffers, later joined by management representatives, formed a Professional Excellence Committee to enhance their effectiveness and technical excellence while at the same time taking a more active role in the improvement of their company. At their first meeting they brainstormed the issues that needed to be addressed. The final list of issues was assigned to committees, which reported back. Another brainstorming session was held to arrive at solutions.[7]

Federal Express initiated its quality improvement process (QIP) in order to ensure prompt delivery of packages and otherwise improve operations. Quality actions teams, established in each of its eleven divisions to identify and solve problems, used brainstorming to address these issues.[8]

AT&T established a brainstorming project to help identify its strategic thrust for the next century.[9] The results were critical to the development of corporate strategy.

A group of five faculty members and three administrators from the Crummer Graduate School of Business at Rollins College brainstormed, seeking to improve the marketing of the school's three MBA programs: professional, full-time, and executive. Over 300 ideas were generated in three forty-minute sessions (one session for each of the three programs). The results included the filming of a videotape, which was sent to prospective students; revision of promotional literature to include newly selected features; the creation of a council to work more closely with local businesses; and initiation of opportunities for students to contribute to the promotional literature and the video tape.[10]

Jeffrey McElnea, president of Einson Freeman, Inc., an award-winning and highly profitable New Jersey sales promotion agency, describes a modified version of the brainstorming process as a vital component of his firm's success: "For each new campaign, we flash every established [sales promotion] technique onto a screen. Then we go through each alternative and hypothetically try to fit the product to it—just to see what would happen. Then we start to combine and recombine the techniques, and there's where the unique part comes in. New techniques are created by synthesizing the old." In one of the agency's award-winning campaigns, "The Smaller the Better Sweepstakes," contestants had to walk into a store and listen to the new Sony Super Walkman to find out whether they had won a prize.[11]

One Southern Bell manager uses case situations to counter the adverse impact of personalities in brainstorming problem-solving situations. She poses the problem in the form of a case. As moderator, she rewards participation but not ideas, thus avoiding a reward-seeking environment.

Most major Japanese firms use some version of brainstorming. For example, Honda engineers attribute a major breakthrough in engine design to a brainstorming exercise that resulted in a 35 percent jump in fuel efficiency in the 1992 Civic VX.[12]

SUMMARY OF STEPS

1. Select a group consisting of six to twelve people, a leader and a recorder.
2. The leader defines the problem for the group, preferably in advance of the brainstorming session.
3. The group suggests solutions to the problem in an interactive format, following the four rules of brainstorming:
   a. No judgments are made about any suggestion.
   b. All ideas, even absurd or impractical ones, are welcome.
   c. Quantity of ideas is a major objective, since it leads to quality.
   d. Ideas may be combined, refined, and piggybacked.
4. After twenty-five to thirty-five minutes, the group takes a break and then returns to critique the ideas.

U.S. Variations on Brainstorming

There are a number of variations on the basic brainstorming technique. Many of the techniques described in this book use some of the elements of brainstorming. Two of the formal variations on brainstorming derived in the U.S. are Take Five and the Crawford Slip Method. These will be discussed later in the chapter.

Japanese Creativity Techniques

Most Japanese creativity techniques are derived from some form of brainstorming.[13] These approaches to problem solving serve the group-oriented Japanese quite well. Western-style brainstorming, with its requirement of verbally tossing out ideas as they are thought of, does not serve the Japanese as well. Being more reserved than people of other nationalities and reluctant to dispute the opinions of others, the Japanese do not often express their thoughts openly. They have developed several variations of brainstorming, each in its own way aimed at adapting the creative power of the process to create a culturally acceptable technique.

発想

Hassoo
Generating
Breakthroughs

These techniques are often used in a creativity circle, which has evolved from the more familiar quality circle. When problems cannot be solved quickly using the conventional techniques (usually quality control), the circle turns to creative processes. The creativity circle involves a work group trying to solve problems together in a creative manner. The brainstorming involved in such circles tends to be incremental in nature and focused on a particular issue. Participants would be asked to think of new ideas for solving the problem before coming to the next circle meeting. This they might do on the weekends, at home, on the train on the way home after work, or over drinks with colleagues.

Participants present their ideas to the circle (usually anonymously, in writing), where they are analyzed for their potential use in solving the problem at hand. If the ideas are presented verbally, the group's comments will be made after a period of time for reflection, and often after hearing some of the responses of others, with time set aside for piggybacking on those. Four Japanese variations on brainstorming are described later in this chapter: Lotus blossom technique (MY), Mitsubishi method, NHK method, and TKJ method. These techniques can be used in U.S. organizations without changing any of their components or with adjustments as the user sees fit.

66/2. BRAINWRITING

Brainwriting is a form of non-oral brainstorming to which the basic brainstorming rules apply. Participants, sitting in a circle, write down their ideas for solving a given problem and pass their papers to their neighbors in the circle, who then brainstorm the ideas for a specified period, say five minutes, and then pass the papers on to the next person. The purpose here is to help you build on the ideas of others, to improve them. Three exchanges are usually enough to produce a lot of good ideas. The leader can then read the ideas, have them written on the board, and so on, direct the group to repeat the brainstorming exercise if necessary.[14] The principal advantage of brainwriting is that the leader is unlikely to influence participants unduly. The main disadvantage is the lack of spontaneity. I like to have the first person prepare three columns for the 1st, 2nd and 3rd person's ideas so that we can find out how the solution progressed from person to person. The first set of ideas usually takes only about two minutes and the later rounds take more time because participants have to read the other peoples' ideas before adding their own.

101
CREATIVE
PROBLEM
SOLVING
TECHNIQUES

125

SUMMARY OF STEPS

1. The problem is identified.
2. Participants, sitting in a circle, write down their ideas for solving the problem.
3. After a specified period, participants pass their ideas on to the next person in the circle.
4. This person then piggybacks on the original solutions to develop new ones, writing them on the same piece of paper.
5. Three or more iterations occur.
6. Ideas are read aloud, written on a white board, or discussed and evaluated in some other way.

67/3. BRAINWRITING POOL

This is one of the techniques developed at the Battelle Institute in Frankfurt, Germany. A group of six to eight people sitting around a table write down their ideas about a given problem. As soon as a participant has written down four ideas, that person may put his or her paper in the middle of the table. However, people are allowed to continue writing down their ideas without being obliged to pass their papers to the center. When participants run out of ideas they exchange their paper for one from the middle of the table and produce new ideas by piggybacking on the ideas listed there. Eventually all participants should exchange their paper for one of those in the brain pool.

The session should go on for about half an hour.[15]

This method gives participants freedom to continue with their own thoughts rather than forcing them to add to the thoughts of others.

SUMMARY OF STEPS

1. The problem is identified.
2. A group of six to eight people, sitting around a table, write their solutions to the problem on a piece of paper.
3. After writing down at least four ideas, each person places his or her piece of paper in the center of the table.
4. When participants run out of ideas, they may choose one of the slips of paper from the center of the table and piggyback on those ideas to create new ones.
5. Eventually every participant should exchange his or her piece of paper for one in the center of the table.

DILLARD DEPARTMENT STORES USES PRICING AND TECHNOLOGY TO BEAT THE COMPETITION

A lot of so-called industry experts didn't give Dillard Department Stores much of a chance to succeed when it came time to compete in the big leagues. Oh its strategy was ok for the back-water towns where it originated, but not in the big cities. Nothing could have been further from the truth. Dillard understands the needs of the 1990s consumer, and satisfies those needs. It provides moderate to high priced goods at reasonable prices, and provides convenience, service and quality. Technologically based process innovations are a major ingredient in Dillard's success. It uses an on line information system networked to every company point-of-sale register to track purchases, inventory levels and sales person performance. Several times a day, company executives search the company's information base to see if Liz Claiborne's new line is selling as well in Dallas as had been anticipated, or to determine how many pairs of a new shoe style were sold in Orlando.

Salesperson performances are tracked by computer. Those who meet quotas receive rasies. The company works to improve the performances of those who don't. Continued failure to meet quotas results in dismissal. Managers too are judged by sales. Sales managers spend a lot of time walking the floor and talking to customers like Marcie McCauley of St. Louis who considers herself the "queen of shoppers." When she wanted to buy her husband some shirts, she chose Dillard. Why, "because they always have the selection I want." Marcie continues, "They carry a lot of brands other Midwestern stores don't have and the largest shoe selection (50,000 pair) I've ever seen." Dillard's sophisticated information system helps make such inventories possible. The firm knows what is selling and what will sell.

Dillard's technology also enables it to get merchandise into stores quickly. Most stores call or write their vendors to restock certain items, but using electronic data interchange with 187 of its suppli-

CONTINUES ON PAGE 128

DILLARD
Continued from page 127

ers, the firm is able to get inventory restocked in 12 days or less. These firms tap into Dillard's information network, track inventory levels, and give Dillard preferential treatment in refilling orders. "We'll jump through hoops to do business with them," says Leonard Rabinowitz, president of women's apparel maker, Carol Little. The firm did $50 million in business with Dillard in 1991, up from nothing five years previously. Rabinowitz likes working with Dillard. "They have really good communications with their key vendors. If I have a problem, I can pick up the phone and discuss it with (president) Bill Dillard and he'll handle it on the spot."

Finally, Dillard has a uniquely innovative centralized approach to managing that defies many of the books on management. Unlike most retailers who centralize accounting and legal functions only, Dillard also centralizes advertising, catalogs and merchandise buying. The key to its success is that it distributes the merchandise according to a store's individual needs. One store manager observes, "If you need more merchandise in your store, or more sales help, you never have to beg for it or try to convince them with a 10-page memo. You just make a phone call."

Source: Carol Hymowitz and Thomas F. O'Boyle, "A Way that Works: Two Disparate Firms Find Keys to Success in Troubled Industries," *Wall Street Journal*, May 29, 1991, pp. A1, A7.

68/4. BRAINWRITING 6-3-5

There are a number of variations of brainwriting developed at the Battelle Institute in Frankfurt, Germany. They include brainwriting pool, brainwriting 6-3-5, gallery method, pin card technique, and the SIL method. The name of this method is derived from the fact that six people produce three new ideas in three columns within five minutes.[16] After five minutes the paper is passed on to the next person, who adds his or her variations to these ideas. This process is repeated six times until all the participants have contributed to all the papers. Theoretically, within thirty minutes the group can produce 108 ideas; realistically, by the time you allow for duplications, perhaps sixty good ideas emerge. Still, this is a very productive effort.

You might want to modify this process so that less time is given in the beginning and more at the end for each iteration. The first set of ideas usually takes only about two minutes and the later rounds take more time because participants have to read the other peoples' ideas before adding their own.

SUMMARY OF STEPS

1. The problem is identified.
2. Six people, sitting in a circle, write down three ideas in three columns within a specified time.
3. Participants then pass their ideas on to the next person in the circle.
4. This person piggybacks on the original solutions and develops new ones, writing these beneath the solutions offered by the previous person.
5. The process is repeated until every person has contributed to every other person's original thoughts.
6. The results are discussed and evaluated.

69/5. CREATIVE IMAGING

This technique is often used in creativity and innovation programs. It is based on the assumption that developing visualization skills improves creativity.[17]

Creative imaging consists of three steps: envisioning a specific need for change, envisioning a better way, and formulating a vision-based plan of action. The exercise can be done

101
CREATIVE
PROBLEM
SOLVING
TECHNIQUES

129

by individuals and the resulting images provided to the group, or it can be guided by a leader/facilitator in a group setting.

The size of the group is best limited to six or eight people, although more can be accommodated. A typical use of the process is to ask a group of corporate participants to describe where they "see" the corporation ten years from now in an ideal world. Since the key to successful use of the techinque is to get the members of a group to respond to their visions, facilitation skills are especially important. In order to inspire group members to feel free to let their imaginations run wild, the facilitator must encourage them to shed their inhibitions.

A consideration that tends to limit the applicability of the technique is the fact that, according to neurolinguistic theory, while many people (60 to 80 percent of the population) are "visuals," the remainder are "verbals," and "feelers."[18] If a person is not in the "visual" category, he or she won't feel comfortable with this exercise unless the facilitator succeeds in presenting the concept attractively and convincingly.

70/6. CREATIVE LEAPS

Creative imaging is one of four techniques that are collectively know as creative leaps.[19] The creative leap is a powerful method for developing breakthrough concepts. It occurs when the group jumps to idealistic solutions, then moves back in time to prepare a plan to make them happen, solving problematic issues as it goes.

There are four primary ways in which a company or group can train itself to take creative leaps:

1. Creating a description of what it wants the company to be like in the future.
2. Creating a description of the ideal competitor in the future.

3. Visualizing the ideal products of the future, those that could be created if there were no technical or financial constraints.

4. Determining the information the company needs to win.

The limitations described in the section on creative imaging apply. The facilitator needs to be skilled in unleashing imagination in a group situation.

71/7. CREATIVITY CIRCLES

Quality circles are small groups of workers who meet to solve quality problems related to their specific work areas. First developed in Japan, quality circles have helped Japanese firms achieve superior quality compared to their competitors. Recently the concept has been expanded under the banner of "creativity circles" to include all types of problems, not just quality problems, and to incorporate a number of group as well as individual creativity processes. Such modifications have occurred in both Japan and Europe.[20] In Japan they were a natural extension of the quality circle as the need for more creative solutions to problems became apparent. Creativity circles are not yet well understood or utilized in the United States. However, Japanese and European firms are utilizing them quite successfully. This chapter describes group creativity processes that managers can use in their work groups to improve performance by raising levels of creativity and innovation. If your organization seeks to improve group creativity, it should use the techniques described here to turn quality circles into creativity circles.

101
CREATIVE
PROBLEM
SOLVING
TECHNIQUES

131

72/8. CRAWFORD SLIP METHOD

In 1925 C. C. Crawford of the University of Southern California invented the Crawford slip method (CSM), a type of brainstorming.[21] The name is derived from the use of slips of paper, about the size of note cards, on which participants write their ideas. A CSM group may consist of any number of people, but larger groups are desirable since the time allotted for generating ideas is short—normally about ten minutes. About 400 ideas should be produced by a group of 20 people in a thirty- to forty-minute period. The process consists of four key steps.

STEP I

The facilitator creates target or focus statements. These are statements that help draw responses from participants. Targets must be carefully constructed. Most idea generation methods simply state a problem. In CSM, a problem area related to an issue is identified and an overall problem is stated. Then additional statements are made that further define the problem. Two representative target statements are shown in Tables 5.1 and 5.2.

STEP 2

Participants then write their replies on slips of paper, using one slip for each idea. The slips are small (4 1/4 by 2 3/4 inches) to ensure that answers are concise and clearly written. (This size also helps ease data reduction in later steps of the process.) [Notecards will suffice.]

In writing their responses, participants follow specific rules:

- Write across the long edge, not across the end of the slip.
- Write on the very top edge of the slip.
- Write only one sentence per slip.
- Use a new slip for explanations.
- Avoid words like "it" or "this."
- Write out acronyms the first time they are used.
- Write short sentences using simple words.
- Write for people outside your field.
- Write until time is called.

TABLE 5.1 Target A

TQM Implementation Problems: (Problem Area)
Where is the System Lacking? (Overall Problem)

- What is less than perfect in the way TQM is implemented?
- What difficulties do you and your colleagues have in implementing TQM?
- What are the roadblocks, bottlenecks, delays, and frustrations you have experienced while implementing TQM?
- Write each trouble, failure, waste, fraud, or abuse related to TQM implementation on a separate slip.

Source: Janet Fiero, "The Crawford Slip Method," *Quality Progress* (May 1992), pp. 40, 41.

TABLE 5.2 Target B

Advice to Decision Makers: (Problem Area)
How to Implement TQM? (Overall Problem)

- Remedies are the flip side of problems
- Provide your best recommendations for eliminating or alleviating the troubles you just identified.
- What different policies, approaches, or procedures have you used or seen used that worked well?
- If you had complete control, how would you change things for the better?
- Write any first ideas on a slip—don't wait for the optimum solution
- Write each remedy for implementing TQM on a separate slip.

Source: Janet Fiero, "The Crawford Slip Method," *Quality Progress* (May 1992), pp. 40, 41.

101
CREATIVE
PROBLEM
SOLVING
TECHNIQUES

133

Participants are then thanked for their inputs and usually dismissed. In most cases participants do not take part in the data reduction process. (CSM is similar to the TKJ method described later in this chapter except that in the TKJ method participants help in the data reduction process.) Participants are, however, given a summary of the results.

STEP 3

The facilitator performs data reduction, which consists of the following steps:

1. Sort the slips into many general categories.

2. Consolidate these into a few major catergories.

3. Refine these categories and develop an outline for the written report.

4. Compile into chapters, divisions, sections, and paragraphs and edit the written report.

For the Implementing TQM target discussed earlier, four general categories, each with two to four subcategories, emerged: ready, set, go, oops. The subcategories for "go" were training, systems changes, participation, resources.

STEP 4

In writing the final report, all of the related comments on slips are itemized under the relevant subcategory headings. Duplications should be eliminated.

CSM has been used extensively in consulting seminars and projects as well as in total quality management programs for numerous companies and governmental units.

CSM is similar to other techniques involving slips of paper or 3 by 5 cards: the TKJ method and the NHK method (described later in this chapter), the idea bits and racking method, and the 7 x 7 method (both described in Chapter 4). Various procedures for sorting, collecting, revising inputs, and so forth could be adapted to the method. For example, you might want to add a visual presentation stage in which participants piggyback on the ideas. You might also want to use cards as starting points for a brainwriting session.

73/9. DELPHI TECHNIQUE

The traditional Delphi process used in scenario forecasting can be employed in generating alternatives in much the same manner as individual brainstorming.[22] In the Delphi process a questionnaire, based on some perception of a situation, is mailed or otherwise communicated to experts in the field. Their individual responses are collected, and summarized, and the summaries are returned to each expert with instructions to revise his or her responses as necessary. The process continues through a series of iterations until a general consensus is reached. Participants whose responses deviate widely from those of the other participants are required to submit justifications for the disparity. These too are summarized and distributed to the others.

The Delphi technique is especially useful in situations in which it is important to separate the ideas of individuals from those of others yet to collect them into a combined set produced by an "expert" group. It is a noninteractive group technique by design, but interaction does in fact occur. Thousands of major Delphi studies have been carried out in many disciplines and in various societies. For example, the technique has been used to identify the ten most important issues of the 1990s in human resources management,[23] future trends in logistics management,[24] and the expected levels of tourism in Singapore.[25]

This is an excellent technique for pooling the ideas of geographically separated experts. All participants have an equal chance to make a contribution, and the ideas are judged on their merits, not on their sources. Moreover, ideas are not influenced by individual or group persuasion. There are

101
CREATIVE
PROBLEM
SOLVING
TECHNIQUES

135

some disadvantages, however. The process is time-consuming and requires a high degree of motivation over a long period. It lacks the piggybacking effect and spontaneity of brainstorming and other interactive group processes, affording no chance for verbal clarification of meanings. Success depends on the analyst's ability to make creative use of the results of his or her study, to facilitate the creativity of expert participants, and to write questionnaires.

SUMMARY OF STEPS

1. Forecasters prepare a questionnaire based on their perception of the situation.
2. This is mailed to a group of experts, who respond to the questionnaire.
3. Individual responses are collected and summarized.
4. Summaries are returned to respondents for their reaction.
5. The process continues until a general consensus is reached.

74/10. EXCURSION TECHNIQUE

The excursion technique was originally introduced as part of synectics, a process described later in this chapter. However, it can and should be used by itself. The excursion technique is especially useful when the group has not arrived at a solution to a problem even after using other creative processes such as brainstorming or storyboarding. It can be used for either narrowly defined or complex problems, but it probably works best on a more narrowly defined problem for which a conceptual breakthrough is needed. It has been slightly modified here from its original description so as to make it more functional.

The Process

There are four major steps in the excursion process: the excursion itself, the drawing of analogies between the problem and the events in the excursion, the analysis of these analogies to see what creative understanding or solutions can occur, and the sharing of experiences with the group.

1. The Excursion. The leader instructs each member of the group to take an imagined excursion into or through some physical location that has nothing to do with the problem at hand. Normally the leader asks participants to close their eyes and use their imagination for this journey, which may be through a museum, a jungle, a city, or any other kind of place, real or imagined. For example, a Star Trek journey through space and to unknown planets is popular with some problem solvers.[26] The ability to let go and create visual images is critical to the success of this part of the exercise. If the leader is not confident that all members of the group have this ability, he or she might offer some brief instruction and encourage people to give them imagination free rein. Participants are asked to write down what they see during their excursion. The excursion itself need not last more than five or ten minutes, but it is important for participants to record detailed descriptions of what they see. I recommend that they draw three columns on their papers and write what they saw on their excursion in the first column. If they prefer, group members can record as they go rather than after the excursion is finished.

2. Drawing Analogies. When the excursion period is over, the leader asks participants to take ten to fifteen minutes to draw analogies between what they saw during the excursion and the problem as defined. Participants are not limited to analogies; they can express the relationships between their visual images and the problem in other ways if they wish. They write their analogies or other relationships in the second column opposite each of the items they saw.

3. Evaluating and Understanding. Now the leader asks the participants to determine what the relationships determined in step 2 really mean

101
CREATIVE
PROBLEM
SOLVING
TECHNIQUES

137

in terms of the problem, that is, how understanding these relationships can be used to solve the problem. This is the really challenging part of the process. It requires intuition, insight, and quite often, luck. Participants write their solutions in the third column.

4. Sharing Experiences. Participants are asked to share their excursions, analogies, understandings, and solutions with the group. As with brainstorming, members may piggyback on the ideas of others.

Examples of the Process

A member of a group of bank personnel officers who were experiencing conflicts with other departments described part of her excursion through a natural history museum as follows: "I saw Indians making war on another village. The analogy is obvious. We are at war with the other departments. This tells me just how serious our problem is. I never quite realized it, but, in a way, we are at war and serious measures must be taken to end this feuding before somebody gets killed." Another member of the group found her tour taking her past the section of the museum where rock formations were shown. The various layers of hard and soft rock meant essentially the same thing to her that the Indian warfare had meant to the other woman. When asked how to solve the problem, she said, "We have to take some dynamite (i.e., strong measures) to blow up the hard rock layers separating the departments."

Other analogies are less obvious. One facilitator had worked with NASA personnel for some time to develop a satisfactory device for fastening a space suit. After trying several standard techniques for generating ideas, he had group members take an imaginary excursion through a jungle. One man described his experience as "being clawed at by weeds, trees, and bushes." While describing his experience, he clutched his hands together with his fingers interlaced. While he himself had not made much of his analogy, when the group discussed it they commented on the clutching of his hands. This suggested the overlapping clutching of a Velcro strip and eventually led to the utilization of a Velcro-like fastener for the spacesuit.[27]

Observations on the Technique

The excursion technique is especially useful for a problem that has proved abnormally difficult to solve or calls for really unique solutions as, for example, in developing an advertising campaign or creating product differentiation features in a mature market. The leader needs to encourage participants to let go and to share their experiences. When the process is well explained and understood and participants are properly motivated, really good ideas should emerge.

SUMMARY OF STEPS

1. The leader instructs participants to visualize an excursion into or through some physical location that has nothing to do with the problem at hand.
2. Participants draw analogies between what they saw and the problem.
3. The leader asks participants to determine what the analogies they drew in step 2 suggest in terms of solving the problem.
4. Participants share their experiences and solutions.

75/11. GALLERY METHOD

This is another of the techniques developed at the Battelle Institute in Frankfurt, Germany. In this method, instead of the ideas changing    places, the idea generators change places. The gallery concept receives its name from the fact that each member of a group take a different work area and creates a "gallery" of ideas for others to view.[28] The ideas are presented on flip charts or white board surfaces. After a half hour or so the group members tour each other's galleries and take notes. Participants should not know who worked where. Five minutes are allowed for viewing each gallery and taking notes. Participants then return to their own work areas and add to their lists. The ideas can be summarized later.

101
CREATIVE
PROBLEM
SOLVING
TECHNIQUES

139

A variation of this technique, known as the idea-gallery, allows members to roam from place to place at will, adding their ideas to those displayed.[29]

76/12. GORDON/LITTLE TECHNIQUE

This technique was designed by William Gordon at the Arthur D. Little consulting firm.[30] It was specifically designed to address the difficulties some people have in coping with abstract concepts. When problem solvers are too close to the problem to see the forest for the trees, they can only think of trite and obvious solutions, and fail to suggest creative ideas. And while several other techniques in this book can be used to overcome that problem, especially those that use associations, this technique is especially effective at bringing problem solvers "out of the woods."

The leader/facilitator describes the problem to the participants in decreasing levels of abstraction. Solutions are given at each level. As the description becomes more concrete and less abstract, more specific solutions, but not necessarily better ones, emerge. The solutions from the earlier levels of abstraction can be used to trigger new solutions as the problem becomes more concrete.

Suppose that the problem is how to eliminate personnel through staff reduction. The first level of abstraction might be "How can we make more money?" A second level of abstraction might be "How can we cut costs?" A third level might be "What options are available in cutting costs of personnel?"

This technique requires a strong, flexible leader who can encourage and motivate members of a group to broaden their perspectives and think big.

77/13. GROUP DECISION SUPPORT SYSTEMS

Group decision support systems are software or hardware systems that assist groups in making better decisions. They greatly enhance the ability of groups to work together creatively. Some of these systems enable groups to be more creative and innovative. Most of them, however, seek to improve group dynamics for already existing creativity pro-

cesses. For example, brainstorming and the nominal group technique can be improved by hardware features such as video projection screens and individual and partner computer terminals, which display and score individual inputs for all participants to view.[31]

Wilson Learning Systems of Minneapolis, Minnesota, offers a sophisticated software package for voting on brainstormed issues. Participants can quickly learn the status of any issue from bar charts and other graphic displays.[32] The University of Arizona's Center for the Management of Information offers advanced hardware for facilitating group creative decision processes. The university has two "electronic brainstorming" rooms, each of which has large computer-generated wall screens and individual/partner computer terminals. Participants in brainstorming sessions can enter ideas to be shared with others without making known their source. Sophisticated software is used to record idea generation, voting, and so on, on large video projection screens for all participants to view.[33]

101
CREATIVE
PROBLEM
SOLVING
TECHNIQUES

141

78/14. IDEA BOARD

The idea board is an ongoing problem-solving exercise in which a problem is displayed on a board or wall where members of a group may add thoughts written on note cards.[34] They may also rearrange the cards, provide columnar headings as necessary, and contribute through spontaneous or formally arranged group discussion. One person is responsible for writing problems on the board for members to respond to, keeping the idea cards orderly, and establishing a time deadline. The ideas collected in this way are summarized, and feedback is given to all involved. Non-group members may be allowed to contribute.

This is a useful mechanism if the problem isn't particularly pressing. It has the advantage of getting everyone involved and having a proprietary interest in the solutions that emerge.

79/15. IDEA TRIGGERS

Props or idea triggers are extremely useful for generating ideas. Give participants something tangible to work with that is somehow related to the problem. For example, when product development consultant Steve Kange was hired to help problem solvers invent new flavors of Life Savers, he gave them a list of 75 Baskin-Robbins ice cream flavors, samples of exotic fruits (kiwis, kumquats) and samples of perfumes. The result—the problem solvers came up with Life Savers' very successful "Fruit Juicers" line.[35]

80/16. INNOVATION COMMITTEE

In this technique, managers, technical representatives, and other employees meet periodically to solve problems.[36] Employees bid for the job of coordinator by submitting proposals. The idea is that the better the proposal the more committed the employee, and the more committed the employee the more will get done. Intuit, the microcomputer software firm that makes Quicken, a program that allows consumers and small businesses to write checks and keep track of them on a personal computer, uses the innovation ideas committee to improve productivity and products.

142

81/17. INTERCOMPANY INNOVATION GROUPS

In the intercompany innovation group, top executives from various companies, led by an innovation consultant, meet for the purpose of solving company problems in innovative ways.[37] Other activities of the group may include seminars, study trips to other organizations, and forecasting trends in major environmental factors. Such groups are quite popular in Europe, especially Norway and Denmark, and are becoming more common in the United States.

82/18. LION'S DEN

The Lion's Den is a lambs versus the lions group problem solving session.[38] At the beginning of a normal meeting of a department, or a meeting among departments, the work group designated to present a problem, the lambs, makes its pitch to the other members of the group, the lions. Groups rotate into the lamb position periodically and are given at least a week to prepare a problem statement, phrased as "How can we ...?" The problem is drawn as a picture on a flipchart or white board. The lions have the right to refuse the problem as too frivolous, in which case the lambs must work another week on a new problem. The lambs are given five minutes to describe the solutions they propose. The lions then offer feedback, additional solutions, and so on for twenty minutes.

101
CREATIVE
PROBLEM
SOLVING
TECHNIQUES

143

83/19. LOTUS BLOSSOM TECHNIQUE, OR THE MY (MATSUMURA YASUO) METHOD

Yasuo Matsumura, president of Clover Management Research in Chiba City, Japan, developed this technique, drawing upon the idea of a lotus blossom but adding mechanics similar to those of the spreadsheet program Lotus 1.2.3. [39] The petals of a lotus blossom cluster around a central core and spread out from that point. By creating windows similar to those used in spreadsheets, portions of an idea board can be sectioned off in such a way that a central theme is used to derive ideas in surrounding windows, which in turn become the centers of new sets of windows. The process goes like this:

1. A central theme, idea, problem, issue, etc., is written in the center of the MY lotus blossom diagram. (See Figure 5.1.)

2. Participants are then asked to think of related ideas or applications or solutions, issues, and so forth. These ideas are then written into the circles located in the center of the diagram and surrounding the central theme (labeled A through H in Figure 5.1).

3. These ideas then become the basis for generating additional lotus diagrams. For example, A would have a set of eight boxes surrounding it. So would B, C, and so on.

This method serves the Japanese culture well, especially when it comes to generating new applications of existing technologies or products, something the Japanese excel at. U.S. firms would do well to emulate their efforts.

An example of how this technique might be used follows: Assuming that the central theme is superconductivity and the issue is commercial applications, then items to go into circles A through H might include magnetic levitation trains, energy storage, electrical transmission, and computer board wiring. If electrical transmission was written in circle A, it would also be the core theme for the box immediately below circle A. Participants would then be asked to think of eight applications of superconductivity in electrical transmission, and these would then be written in the eight boxes, labeled 1 through 8, that surround the second circled A. The process can then be replicated using each of these eight items.

I have found this technique to be very useful for creating future scenarios. Participants like the way ideas flow rapidly from one set of boxes to another, from one lotus petal to another. This technique combines the free flow of the mind map, described in Chapter 4, with the structure of the storyboard, described later in this chapter.

Figure 5.1 The Lotus Blossom

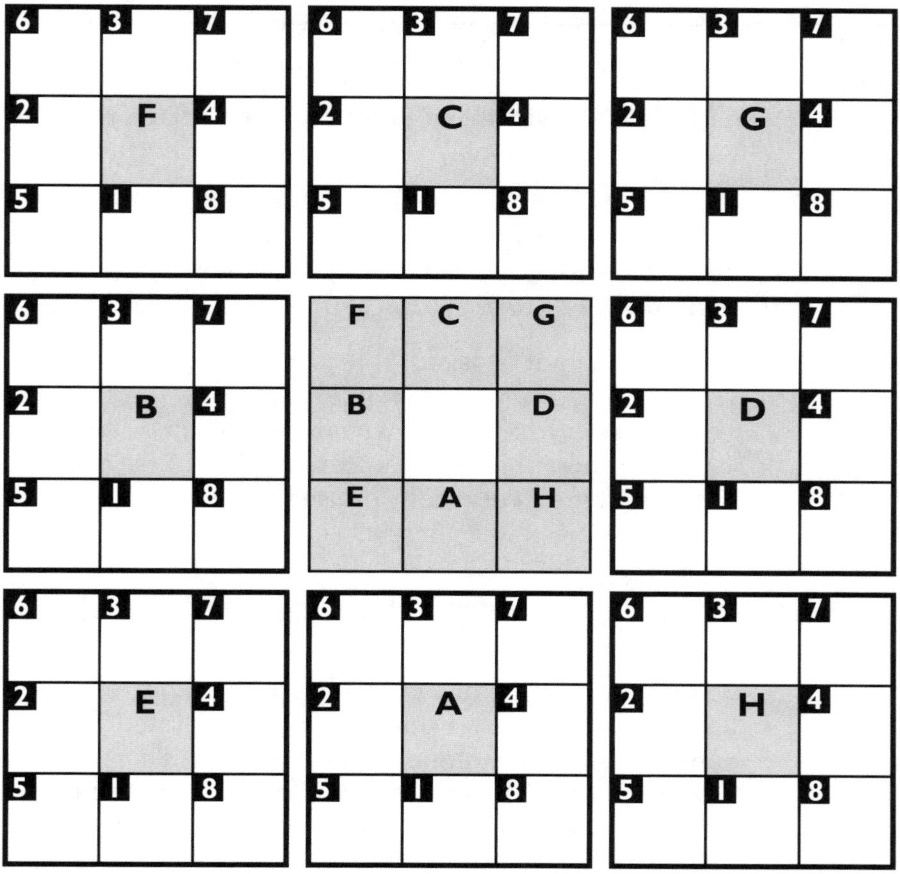

101
CREATIVE
PROBLEM
SOLVING
TECHNIQUES

145

84/10. MITSUBISHI BRAINSTORMING METHOD

Sadami Aoki of Mitsubishi Resin has developed a Japanese alternative to traditional Western-style brainstorming.[40] It follows these steps:

1. Participants are given a chance to warm up by writing down their ideas before sharing them with others. This step may take fifteen minutes or longer.

2. Each participant is asked to read his or her ideas aloud, volunteering to do so as he or she chooses. Participants are encouraged to write down new ideas that build on the ideas of others that have been read aloud. Participants who didn't have very many original ideas at first can wait and read aloud their piggybacked ideas along with their original ones.

   This reading aloud is similar to what occurs in the U.S.-developed nominal group technique described later. And it has become part of the Mitsubishi method for essentially the same reason that it was incorporated into the nominal group technique: to keep aggressive personalities from dominating a session. But there are important differences, as you will note after you have compared it to the nominal group technique.

3. For the next hour or longer, participants explain their ideas in detail to the group. A group leader creates an "idea map" on a large writing surface, detailing the inputs of

the group. This allows all to apprehend visually the ideas presented and, in most cases, their interrelationships. The Japanese appear to be much more visually oriented than their U.S. counterparts, and this has helped them improve their creativity. *Most authors on creativity agree that members of U.S. organizations need to improve their visualization skills in order to become more creative.*

4. Analysis of inputs proceeds from this point with appropriate attention to the cultural environment. In Japan, this means that comments must be phrased so as to allow others to "save face."

SUMMARY OF STEPS

1. The problem is identified.
2. Participants write down their solutions.
3. Participants read their ideas aloud.
4. Those with no or only a few original ideas can read piggybacked ideas as well as their own.
5. Ideas are explained aloud and in detail.
6. An idea map is drawn.
7. Ideas are discussed and evaluated in a face-saving manner.

85/21. MORPHOLOGICAL ANALYSIS

Morphological analysis was developed by Fritz Zwicky. As you can see in Figure 5.2 it involves a matrix. On the vertical axis are listed particular characteristics, adjectives, adverbs, prepositions, and the like. On the horizontal axis appears another set of objectives, characteristics, factors, adjectives, adverbs, verbs, and so on. The purpose of the analysis is to force one set of characteristics and words against another to create new ideas. Typically, problem characteristics may be listed on one of the axes and a verbal, prepositional, or relational checklist on the other. But any number of factors may be placed on either axis. The important point is to choose factors that may provide new insights into the problem, object, or other focus of the problem-solving effort. In a three-dimensional matrix, a third set of factors can be used.

The advantage of morphological analysis is that numerous ideas can be generated in a short period. A 10 x 10 matrix

101
CREATIVE
PROBLEM
SOLVING
TECHNIQUES

147

yields 100 ideas. A 10 x 10 x 10 matrix yields 1000 ideas. The process is usually done in groups, but it may be done individually first and then developed into a pooled matrix by a leader who incorporates individual inputs. Alternatively, the group may brainstorm the analysis together. Or, the process may be done individually without the involvement of a group.[41]

Figure 5.2 Morphological Analysis

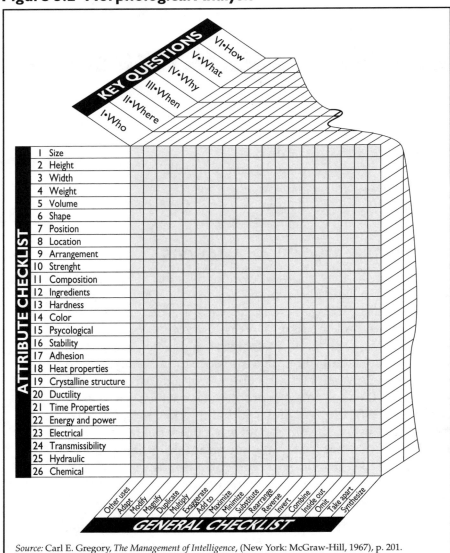

Source: Carl E. Gregory, *The Management of Intelligence*, (New York: McGraw-Hill, 1967), p. 201.

Attributional Morphology

You can list the attributes of a particular object or problem on both axes of a matrix. The resulting cells will be interconnections between the various attributes. Three-D attribute morphology involves listing the attributes on three axes. An exhaustive list of possible combinations will result. The purpose is to generate new types of attributes by using the attributes themselves to trigger thought. As with the other processes described in this book, you want first quantity, then quality. After generating ideas, you reexamine and evaluate the product.

86/22. NHK METHOD

Hiroshi Takahashi developed the NHK method after years of training television production managers at Japan Broadcasting Company (NHK).[42] While it is a lengthy process, it acts like an egg beater, causing ideas to be continually merged and separated, thereby generating new ideas.

SUMMARY OF STEPS

1. In response to a problem statement, participants write down five ideas on separate cards.
2. Participants meet in groups of five. Each person explains his or her ideas to the other members of the group. Other members of the group write down any new ideas that come to mind on separate cards.
3. The cards are collected and sorted into groups by theme.
4. New groups of two or three people are formed. Each group takes one or more of the sorted groups of cards and brainstorms for new ideas related to those on the cards. This lasts for up to half an hour. The new ideas are also written on cards.

CONTINUES ON PAGE 150

5. At the end of this session each group organizes its cards by theme and announces the ideas to the rest of the group. All ideas are written on a large surface by a leader or recorder.
6. Participants are formed into groups of ten and all the ideas on the writing surface are brainstormed, one idea at a time.

87/23. NOMINAL GROUP TECHNIQUE

The nominal group technique (NGT) is a structured small-group process for generating ideas.[43] It can be used to diminish the impact of a dominant person on the outcome of the group's idea generation process, whether the source of the dominance is formal authority or individual personality. The nominal group technique accomplishes this objective through a process that limits an individual's inputs to brief explanations and uses a secret ballot to choose among brainstormed ideas. For this technique to be effective, the participants must agree that the group's decision is binding.

"As a group decision-making process, the nominal group technique is most useful for (1) identifying the critical variables in a specific problem situation; (2) identifying key elements of a program designed to implement a particular solution to some problems; or (3) establishing priorities with regard to problems to be addressed, goals to be attained, desirable end states and so on. In all of these circumstances, it often seems beneficial to aggregate individual judgments into group decisions. However, NGT is not

particularly well suited for routine group meetings that focus primarily on coordination of activities or an exchange of information. Nor is it appropriate for negotiating or bargaining situations."[44]

As with brainstorming, the NGT uses a group of six to twelve people. The leader is also the secretary and records the group's responses, at the appropriate time, on a sizable writing surface that is visible to all participants.

The process of decision making using the nominal group technique consists of four distinct steps, which can be adapted to special conditions as suggested in the following paragraphs.

Step 1: Generation of Ideas

The leader phrases the problem, stimulus question or other focal issue for the participants, and writes this on the white board or other writing surface. Group members are given a specified period, usually five to ten minutes, to write their suggested solutions on notecards. This reflective period helps avoid some of the pressure for conformity to a particular person's ideas. Yet there is still a sense of belonging and responsibility.

Step 2: Recording of Ideas

In the second step the ideas generated in step 1 are recorded, in round-robin fashion, on the board. The leader asks each person in turn for the first idea on his or her list that has not yet been presented by someone else. The process continues until every participant has exhausted his or her list of items and all items have been recorded on the board. When a person's list is exhausted, he or she passes when called upon for solutions. The round robin continues until everyone passes. This process emphasizes the equality of ideas and serves to build enthusiasm. It also depersonalizes the ideas presented and helps prevent prejudging. And it helps ensure that no ideas are lost.

101
CREATIVE
PROBLEM
SOLVING
TECHNIQUES

151

Step 3: Clarification of Ideas

Each idea on the list from step 2 is discussed in the order in which it was written down. Typically, the leader points to each item, asking if everyone clearly understands that item. If there are no questions, then the leader moves on to the next item. When a participant seeks clarification of an item, the presenter of the idea is given a brief period of time, normally thirty seconds to one minute, to respond. More time may be given if necessary, but the leader must make certain that these discussions are brief and that they are not used to sell the idea to the other participants. This process continues until all ideas are understood. The purpose of this step is not to reach agreement on the best choices but simply to achieve understanding of what the choices actually call for.

Step 4: Voting on Ideas

A nominal group will often list from 20 to 100 or more ideas. This list must be somehow narrowed down to the "best" choice as determined by the group. There are several ways to proceed at this point, all based on the principle of the secret ballot. The most common voting procedure is for the leader to have each participant write the five ideas he or she considers best on a 3 x 5 card, which is then passed to the leader for tabulation and announcement of scores. Normally, the five to ten "best" choices as determined by secret ballot are then voted on again to determine the one, two, or three best choices.

In both rounds of the voting process, participants rank their five choices (first iteration) and two or three choices (second iteration). In tabulating scores, the most important item should receive the highest score, the least important the lowest. You may choose to use a scale of 1 to 5, 1 to 3, or something similar. Total votes and total scores should be documented for purposes of comparison.[45]

Observations on the Technique

The nominal group technique has proven to be an effective way of preventing dominant individuals from affecting the outcome of group decision processes. The NGT is best used with rather narrowly defined problems. When the problem is more complex, or when it is difficult to arrive at a solution, interactive techniques, especially storyboarding, may be more beneficial.

Experiences with the Process

Many firms use the NGT for a variety of purposes. It has been used to identify difficulties faced by organizational development (OD) professionals in making OD part of organizational strategy,[46] in strategic planning for an integrated information system in a large firm with many divisions,[47] and in developing strategic databases.[48] When the top managers of *Incentive* magazine sponsored an NGT session to create a more formal incentive program for the magazine's editors and production staff, more than fifty ideas were generated. These were later pared down to a small list.[49]

Variations on Nominal Group

The Improved Nominal Group Technique essentially combines Delphi (explained earlier) with NGT. Participants' inputs are submitted in advance of the meeting. This eliminates the identification of the idea with the person submitting it, as happens in the verbal, one-at-a-time scenario used in NGT. It also can involve a change in voting procedure to allow one negative vote to block an idea.[50]

SUMMARY OF STEPS

1. The problem is identified.
2. Participants are given a specified period to write down their solutions to the problem.
3. Ideas are recorded on a large surface in round-robin fashion.
4. As the process continues, participants will eventually pass as all their ideas have been written on the board.
5. The leader goes down the list of ideas, asking if any need clarification. If they do, then the introducer of the idea has 15 to 30 seconds to explain, but not sell, the idea.
6. Participants vote on the ideas by secret ballot. Usually two rounds of voting are necessary.

88/24. PHILLIPS 66 (DISCUSSION 66)

The Phillips 66 method breaks a larger group down into groups of six, plus a leader and a secretary, for the purpose of brainstorming.[51] Its developer, Don Phillips, then president of Hillsdale College, Michigan, recognized that for many people situational factors such as the size of the group and the design of the meeting room, as well as early training, tend to discourage participation. When large groups are broken into smaller ones these factors are overcome, since in small groups individuals are more likely to express ideas that might be suppressed in larger groups.

In the Phillips 66 method each group focuses on a single problem, which should be well worded, concise, and clearly identified. Participants try to arrive at a decision within six minutes.

89/25. PHOTO EXCURSION

Photo excursion uses the same principles as picture simulation (see Chapter 4). Instead of using prepared pictures for stimulation, participants are required to leave the building, walk around the area with a polaroid camera, and take pictures of possible solutions or visual metaphors for the problem.[52] When the group reconvenes, ideas are shared.

90/26. PIN CARD TECHNIQUE

This is another technique developed at the Battelle Institute of Frankfurt, Germany. This German adaptation of brainwriting is based on another German creativity technique known as the metaphor technique. This process is similar to the NHK method and TKJ method which are described as processes 11 and 13 in this chapter. This version of brainwriting allows for structuring of the ideas quickly.[53]

SUMMARY OF STEPS

1. A group of five to eight people sit around a table.
2. Each member writes his or her thoughts about a given problem on cards (one idea per card) using colored magic markers, a different color for each contributor.
3. All completed cards are passed in the same direction.
4. Each participant reads the cards that have been passed to him or her and passes them on to the next person if the ideas seem worthwhile. Ideas that do not appear useful are set aside.
5. The moderator sorts out the cards that make it all the way around the table.
6. These cards are sorted into categories and pinned to a large surface.

91/27. SCENARIO WRITING

Scenario writing involves analyzing information, thinking and writing about scenarios discussing the company's (or an individual's) potential future. An important part of this exercise begins with identifying problems and opportunities that may result from any of the scenarios envisioned and then solving the problems or taking advantage of the opportunities. It is believed that creating scenarios will lead to many suggested solutions.

Scenario writing is a sophisticated technique that requires considerable time and effort. It is the thinking about future possibilities that is important. The scenarios themselves are somewhat secondary. Few managers, professionals, or other employees think they have time to think about the future, but such activity is vital to success.

101
CREATIVE
PROBLEM
SOLVING
TECHNIQUES

155

Figure 5.3 Sample Scenario Summary

Descriptors	SCENARIO A: The Nation's Future is Dominated by the Oil and Gas Economy	SCENARIO B: Oil and Gas Benefits Lead to Restructured National Economy
Global Economic Development	• Persistent Economic Structural Problems • OECD Growth: About 2% • Inflation Higher: Volatile Exchange Rates	• Moderate Growth, Some Progress Toward Restructuring • OECD Growth: 2.5% • Cyclical Swings in Inflation, Exchange Rates
Geopolitical Relations	• Increasing Protectionism • Slowdown/Reversal of Privatization Policies • U.S.-Western Europe Tensions Exploited by the USSR	• Growing International Trade and Cooperation • Gains for Privatization in OECD • Relaxation of East-West Tensions: Increased Trade
Energy Market Structure	• Oil Demand Growth: 1% • Gas Demand Growth: 2% • OPEC Dominance Gains • North Sea, Barents Sea Developments Pushed • COMECON Gas Available	• Oil Demand Growth: 1% • Gas Demand Growth: 2% • Increases in OPEC Power North Sea, Barents Sea Developments Pushed • COMECON Gas Expansion
Oil and Gas Industry Structure	• Strong Upstream Operations Post 1990	• More Strategic Alliances • Greater Push Downstream

National Economy	• National Will: Unsure, Drifting
	• Economic Restructuring:
	  - Few Initiatives Successful
	  - Petroleum Sector Dominant
	• GNP Growth: About 2.5%
		• Moderately Dynamic National Will
		• Economic Restructuring: Balance Between Petroleum and NonPetroleum Sectors
		• GNP Growth: About 2.5%

Technological Change	• Incremental Development: Fragmented Disciplines • Norwegian R&D Spending: 1.5% of GNP with Oil and Gas as No. 1 Priority • Oil and Gas Technology: Focus on E&P Improvement and New Reserves	• Accelerated Progress: Integration of Disciplines • Growth of Norwegian R&D to 2% of GNP, with new Priorities • Oil and Gas Technology: Focus on New Reserves Access

SCENARIO C: The Country Struggles in a Depressed World	SCENARIO D: The Country is Driven Out of Oil Dependence by Global Restructuring
• Severe Economic Structural Problems, Protectionism • OECD Growth: 1.5% • Volatile Inflation (Some Deflation) and Exchange Rates	• Strong Growth, Following Restructuring Adjustments • OECD Growth: 3–3.5% • Relatively Stable Inflation and Exchange Rates
• Volatile Tension-Filled World: Growth in Protectionism, Nationalism • Emphasis on Government Controls • East-West Relations and Trade Deteriorate	• Agreements Resulting from Stable Political Relations • Flourishing of Market-Orientated Policies • COMECON Drawn more into Global Mainstream
• Oil Demand Growth: 0% • Gas Demand Growth: 1% • Struggle for OPEC to Survive • Barents Sea Development Delayed • COMECON Gas Reduced	• Oil Demand Growth: 1% • Gas Demand Growth: 3% • Loss of OPEC Power and Cohesion • North Sea, Barents Sea Development Slowed
• Mergers/Consolidations Multiply • State-Owned Companies Favored by National Policies	• Strategic Shift from Oil to Gas • Privatization of Some State-Owned Operations

• Malaise: Discouraged, Divided
• Economic Restructuring:
  - All Sectors Struggling
  - Govt. Support of Energy Sector
• GNP Growth: 1–1.5%
	• Strongly Dynamic National Will
	• Economic Restructuring:
	  - Most Initiatives Successful
	  - Gas More Important than Oil
	• GNP Growth: 2.5–3%

• Stalled Development: Restrictive, Protectionist Policies
• Norwegian R&D Spending Overall Declines but Spending on Oil and Gas R&D Constant
• Oil and Gas Technology: Focus on Productivity/Cost Control
	• Rapid Progress: Integration, Global Diffusion of Technologies
	• Norwegian R&D at 2–2.5%
	  - Focus on High-tech
	  - Restructuring
	• Oil and Gas Technology: Focus on Gas Conversion, Artificial Intelligence / Imaging

Source: Reprinted from: *Long Range Planning*, vol. 23, no.2., P.R. Stokke, W.K. Ralston, T.A. Boyce, I.H. Wilson, "Scenerio Planning for Norwegian Oil and Gas", pp. 22, Copyright 1990, with kind permission from Pergamon Press Ltd., Headington Hill Hall, Oxford OX3 0BW, U.K.

101
CREATIVE
PROBLEM
SOLVING
TECHNIQUES

157

Scenario writing can be used in solving several types of problems. It is most often used in preparing alternative strategies for various possible future conditions. Typically the scenario forecasts involve analyzing the organization's internal and external environments for information about its projected strengths and weaknesses, its future opportunities and threats (SWOT). The firm is interested in building up strengths and overcoming weaknesses in order to take advantage of opportunities and mitigate threats. Internally, the firm studies factors such as its technology, functional prowess, resources, capabilities, employees, and management. Externally, it examines factors such as competitors' anticipated actions, the expected economy, and the changing nature of customer's buying practices.

Three to five key drivers of the company's future are determined—for example, changing demographics or technology. Future scenarios are then forecast on the basis of the likely impact of these key drivers on from five to ten key factors such as market share, customer responses, buying patterns, the economy, and research and development needs. Each scenario focuses on one or two drivers. For example, if changing technology is seen as critical to a firm's future, a scenario is depicted in which the likely impact of changing technology on the key factors is described. Other scenarios are created using another key driver. Thus, the impacts of an aging population could be described in terms of the same factors—market share, customer responses, buying patterns, the economy, research and development needs, and so on. Figure 5.3 presents a typical summary of four scenario forecasts. These four scenarios were created by Norwegian Oil & Gas in an attempt to understand the future need for oil and gas, and hence their need to drill for oil and gas. From these scenarios, they developed a R & D strategy for oil and gas exploration. Note how the drivers often result in the titles of the scenarios. The scenario writers identify opportunities (and threats) and determine what the company needs in the way of increased strengths and reduced weaknesses to take advantage of those opportunities. Strategies are determined on the basis of this SWOT analysis.[54]

RICOH'S PRODUCT DEVELOPMENT SCENARIOS

Japan's RICOH is one of the world's leading office automation equipment manufacturers. It has the largest market share in electronic copiers, facsimiles, and write-once optical discs. It also makes office computers, Japanese word processors, printers, semi-conductors, cameras and software. RICOH's eight research laboratories receive an unusually high level of support because RICOH believes that creative and innovative research is the key to the company's future. Some of the primary features of its support programs are flexible work hours, special motivation systems, and numerous information exchange efforts. For example, in the center of the primary research building is a community plaza with a giant meeting table in the shape of a tree around which colleagues from different research projects may meet to brainstorm and exchange ideas.

In deciding what to research, RICOH's planners study probable customer needs over a certain time horizon. In determining future customer needs, social and technological trends are investigated and analyzed. Scenarios are then prepared based on these analyses. For example, "The office in the year 2001" would be a typical focal point around which to build scenarios. A scenario might start this way, "One fine morning, Mr. R. got up at 8 a.m. as usual. He sat down on the sofa in front of the wide flat-panel screen. His home computer, connected with his office...." RICOH's planners extract potential products from these scenarios and pick 10-15 per year for research. Next, strategic targets would be broken down into research themes. At this point, researchers join the project. Alternatively, planners may also choose among seed programs that allow researchers to follow projects of interest to them that also have marketability. Next, a research strategy is determined and carried out. Finally, technology transfer occurs between the lab and the factory.

Source: Akira Okamoto, "Creative and Innovative Research at RICOH," *Long Range Planning*, October 1991, p. 13.

THE INNOVATIVE EDGE IN ACTION 5.2

When little time is available, scenario daydreaming may be used. It proceeds in the same basic way as scenario planning, but it seldom results in a sizable written document the way scenario planning does, and there is much less formal research than with scenario planning.[55]

Any problem situation that is changing over time lends itself to using scenarios. Southern California Edison used this technique in planning for new electric production capacity, and determining what actions to take as a result.[56]

SUMMARY OF STEPS

1. Define the problem.
2. Identify three to five drivers of the firm's future.
3. Determine impacts of these on five to ten key factors (including the drivers).
4. Write scenarios based on the key drivers and their impacts on the key factors.
5. Prepare a summary chart.
6. Creativity occurs in writing the scenarios and reacting to them.

92/28. SIL METHOD

This technique was developed at the Battelle Institute in Frankfurt, Germany. The letters SIL form an acronym in German that translates roughly as "successive integration of problem elements."[57] This technique is similar to other versions of brainwriting, many of which were also developed at Battelle.

SUMMARY OF STEPS

1. Each participant silently generates responses to a problem statement.
2. Two group members each read an idea aloud.
3. The other members try to combine the two ideas into one.
4. Another member reads his or her idea aloud and the other members try to combine it with the previous idea.
5. This process continues until a workable solution has been found or the deadline is reached.

93/29. STORYBOARDING

Storyboarding is a structured exercise based on brainstorming.[58] It is extremely flexible and can be readily modified. It assists in all stages of the problem solving process but especially in generating and deciding on alternatives. In contrast to brainstorming, which is best used with a narrowly defined problem, storyboarding is especially useful for solving complex problems. It can be used not only to provide solutions but also to help define the various aspects of a complex problem. A specific format for describing the problem and a specific process for solving it are provided.

Background

Walt Disney and his staff devised a forerunner of the storyboard technique in 1928. Disney wanted to achieve full animation in cartoon features, something no one had been able to accomplish previously. To do so, he produced an enormous number of drawings—thousands more than the then current state of the art required. Approximately four times as many frames per second were to be used to produce high-quality cartoon features, giving his firm a major competitive edge.

101
CREATIVE
PROBLEM
SOLVING
TECHNIQUES

161

Before long, however, piles of drawings were stacked up in the small studio. It was nearly impossible to keep tabs on what had been completed and what still needed to be done. Finally, Disney decided to have his artists pin their drawings on the walls of the studio in sequence. Thereafter anyone could know at a glance how far along any given project was. — The technique saved time; scenes could be discarded with ease; fewer meetings were required. The story was told on a wall covered with a special kind of board; hence the term storyboard.

Mike Vance joined the Disney organization in the 1960s. During his tenure as head of Disney University, the company's employee development program, he and members of his staff refined the storyboard concept. They recognized that the technique had problem-solving potential beyond facilitating the layout of cartoon features. Vance left Disney in the late 1970s to consult full time with firms on the use of storyboarding. It is from his system, as modified by Jerry McNellis and to some extent by me, that the storyboarding process described here has evolved.

An Overview of The Process

Storyboarding is, as it name implies, creating a story on boards. You take your thoughts and those of others and spread them out on a wall as you work on a project or attempt to solve a problem. When you put ideas on storyboards, you begin to see interconnections—you see how one idea relates to another, how all the pieces fit together.

Storyboarding follows the basic processes of brainstorming— it uses a leader, a secretary, and a group of people working openly and following the four rules of brainstorming. However, storyboarding takes brainstorming several steps further. It is more organized and deals with more complex issues.

Storyboarding demands a high level of participation, but once the ideas start flowing, those involved will become immersed in the problem. They will begin to "hitchhike on," or embellish, each other's ideas.

A Story Board on Storyboarding

A storyboard is organized in columns underneath major elements known as headers.

The Topic Header. Figure 5.4 portrays the first step in storyboarding: identifying the topic. At the top of the storyboard, the topic to be defined or the problem to be solved is identified. This is referred to as the topic header. Here the topic header is storyboarding. It could just as easily be "recruiting high-quality employees in a low-skill labor market" or "differentiating our product from those of our competitors."

The Purpose Header. Figure 5.5 indicates the second step in the process, establishing the purpose header and brainstorming the purposes for pursuing the topic, which are then listed beneath the purpose header. These purposes must be identified before any other headers are created. Each item placed under a header is known as a subber. The purpose header in our example has four subbers: solving problems more effectively; raising levels of creativity; improving planning, communication, and organization; and increasing participation. Others may be added later.

The Miscellaneous Header. Figure 5.5 also contains the miscellaneous header. The column beneath this header contains all the items that don't seem to fit in any of the other columns. Items are placed under the miscellaneous header as the rest of the columns are brainstormed. Later they may be placed under another header or may become headers themselves if enough similar items appear in the miscellaneous column. In our example there is only one subber under the miscellaneous header: background. More will be added later.

The Other Headers. Figure 5.6 portrays the third step in the storyboarding process: identification of the other headers— that is, the major issues and/or solutions to the problem, other than the purpose and miscellaneous headers. Brainstorming of the major issues involved in storyboarding reveals the following headers: Major Uses of Storyboarding, Types of Storyboards, Types of Sessions for Each Storyboard, The Project Team, Materials Involved in a Storyboard, Rules for a Creative-Thinking Session, Rules for a Critical-Thinking Session, and The Role of the Leader.

101
CREATIVE
PROBLEM
SOLVING
TECHNIQUES

163

Figure 5.4 Step One of Storyboarding

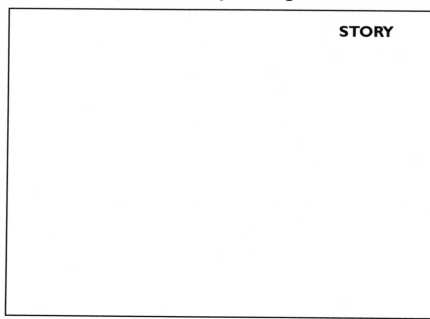

Figure 5.5 Step Two of Storyboarding

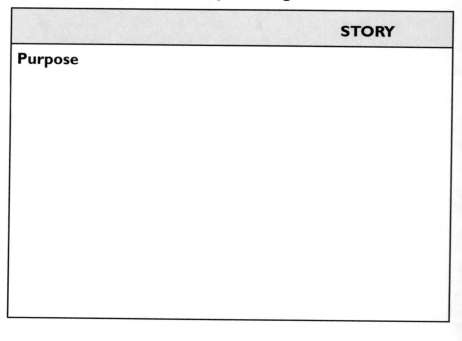

BOARDING

BOARDING

Miscellaneous

101
CREATIVE
PROBLEM
SOLVING
TECHNIQUES

165

Figure 5.6 Step Three of Storyboarding

				STORY
Purpose	**Major Uses**	**Types of Storyboards**	**Types of sessions in a Storyboard**	**The Project Team**
Solve problems more effectively				
Raise levels of creativity				
Improve/ planning, communication				
Increase participation				

Figure 5.7 Step Four of Storyboarding

				STORY
Purpose	**Major Uses**	**Types of Storyboards**	**Types of sessions in a Storyboard**	**The Project Team**
Solve problems more effectively	Strategic problem solving	Planning	Creative thinking	5-8
Raise levels of creativity	Operational problem solving	Ideas	Critical thinking	Composition of group
Improve planning, communication		Communication who, what, when		
Increase participation		Organization how, tasks, who		

BOARDING				
Materials	The Rules for a Creative Thinking Session	The Rules for a Critical Thinking Session	Role of the Leader	Miscellaneous

BOARDING				
Materials	The Rules for a Creative Thinking Session	The Rules for a Critical Thinking Session	Role of the Leader	Miscellaneous
Wall boards	No criticism	Be objective	Choose topic, team	Background:: Disney, Mike Vance
Cards: sizes; colors; pins; tape	Quantity no quality	Be critical	Choose type of storyboard, brief team	Visual
Wide tipped markers	Piggyback ides	Attack ideas not people	Warm up, review rules	Flexible
Post It notes	The wilder the better		Topic header headers subbers	Use symbols
Scissors, string	Quick and dirty		Conduct creative thinking	
Table			Conduct critical thinking	

101
CREATIVE
PROBLEM
SOLVING
TECHNIQUES

167

At an earlier stage there might have been a column labeled "Process," with subbers such as Major Uses of Story Boards, Types of Story Boards, and Types of Story Board Sessions. But further consideration would have shown the need for headers for each of these topics. So in Figure 5.7 headers were created for each of them. This action reveals the flexibility of storyboarding, a characteristic that has been added to the miscellaneous column in Figure 5.7.

Sometimes you may question whether an idea is important enough to be a header. If in doubt, make it a header; later you can make it a subber under another header.

Major Uses of Story Boards. Two subbers are identified: strategic and operational problem solving. Today virtually all problems are of one type or the other. There are few tactical problems left because of the time compression caused by accelerated rates of change, but they could be listed too. These problem-solving efforts can be individual, group, or organizational in nature.

Types of Story Boards. There are four principal types of story boards: planning, ideas, organization, and communication boards.

The Planning Story Board. The first step in the storyboarding process. It contains all the major ideas related to solving the problem described by the topic header. It is the blueprint for the actions that follow. The storyboarding process evolves mostly from the planning board.

The Ideas Story Board. The second step in the storyboarding process. It is an expansion of some of the ideas (hence the name) contained in the planning board. Typically, a header such as Rules for Creative Thinking, would become a topic header in an ideas board, and each of the subbers under that header in the planning board would become headers in the ideas board. Participants brainstorm the subbers for each of these headers and may add headers related to actual solutions of particular problems. Once the ideas board is complete, then the organization board is necessary.

The Organization Story Board. Answers three questions: What are the tasks that need to be done? When do they need to begin? Who will be doing them? It takes the objectives and plans established in the planning and ideas boards and breaks them into individual and group objectives and tasks. I like to write the organization information on the planning and/or ideas boards rather than create a separate board. Your preference may vary. Once the storyboarding sessions are over, this information will need to be transcribed in a detailed format. For this an organization board is useful. Once solutions have been identified and tasks created, a communications board is used to describe how this information will be conveyed.

The Communications Story Board. Answers these questions: Who needs to know? What do they need to know? When do they need to know it? What media are going to be used to convey the information? This board can be completed after the tasks have been established.

Some people prefer to begin work on this board early in the creative-thinking session. I don't. You have to have the tasks established before you can communicate them. As with the organization board, I prefer to simply write on the planning and ideas boards, saving the separate report of this information for later. The beauty of storyboarding is that such flexibility is possible.

STORY BOARD Planning

STORY BOARD Ideas

STORY BOARD Organization

STORY BOARD Communication

You can use planning and ideas boards in all creative-thinking projects---they're the core of the story board system. The extent to which you use communication and organization boards depends on the scope of the project, the size of your organization, the number of people outside the project team who need to know about the project and its progress, and the number of people who will eventually be involved in implementing the ideas.

101
CREATIVE
PROBLEM
SOLVING
TECHNIQUES

169

The Types of Story Board Sessions. There are two types of story board sessions: creative-thinking sessions and critical-thinking sessions. They take place for each of the four types of story boards—planning, ideas, organization, and communication.

Rules for a Creative Thinking Session: During the creative-thinking session the objective is to come up with as many ideas and/or solutions as possible. You follow the basic brainstorming rules: Consider all ideas relevant, no matter how impractical and farfetched they may seem; the more ideas that arise, the better; no criticism is allowed at this point; hitchhike on each others' ideas and keep comments short. (There will be an evaluation session following the creativity session.) Each creative-thinking session should last no longer than an hour (ideally thirty to forty minutes) to maintain maximum interest and effectiveness. The critical-thinking session that follows can be roughly twice as long.

Rules for a Critical Thinking Session: After the planning board has been completed to the group's satisfaction, take a break. Now you're ready for a critical-thinking session. During the critical-thinking session the ideas and solutions generated in the creative-thinking session are evaluated. Now is the time to think judgmentally.

First look at a header. Ask, these questions: Will the idea work? Why is it up there? Is it necessary to our objective? Is it feasible? If the header doesn't stand up in the critical-thinking session, remove it from the board or move it to another position on the board. Then evaluate each subber under the headers (keep in mind that if a header is not valid, it does not mean that any particular subber under it won't work). If a subber no longer seems pertinent or practical, toss it out or move it. Then go on to evaluate the next header and group of subbers under it, and so on until the entire board has been appraised. Your objective is to narrow the list of ideas to something more manageable.

Additional Steps in the Process. The next step is to develop the next board in the sequence. If you are on a planning board, for example, your next step is a creativity session for an ideas board. If you are on an ideas board, you need to hold the creativity session for the organization board.

It is best to schedule the sessions over a few days or weeks, recognizing that people are under time constraints. On the other hand, a lengthy "grind" session sometimes works well and may be necessary if the project is a crisis situation.

The Project Team. Before you conduct a creative problem-solving session using the storyboard system, you must assemble your project team. Normally there are five to eight

101
CREATIVE
PROBLEM
SOLVING
TECHNIQUES

171

participants, but it is feasible to include up to twelve participants. For demonstration purposes, storyboard groups can be very large. There may be times when you'll want to put together a separate project team to work on a particular ideas board. The wider and deeper you can go for ideas, the more productivity and creativity will result.

The members of the group should be chosen carefully. They may come from various levels of the organization or from the same level. They may come from different organizations. They may even be strangers. They may have different or similar backgrounds. For example, you might ask a vice president and a foreman to join your team. You'll want to consider the balance between male and female members and include representatives of minority groups where possible. If power or authority situations might preclude active participation, participants should be drawn from the same level of the organizational hierarchy.

Role of the Leader. The group leader makes sure the team meets on time and that the work gets done. He or she may facilitate the process as well. Because the facilitator's job is so demanding, the group may elect (or the leader may appoint) different facilitators from time to time. Before starting any creative problem solving session, the leader should describe the topic to the team. The leader should be certain everyone understands the subject and why the session is being conducted.

The Role of the Secretary. The secretary records the ideas generated in the creative-thinking session and deletes them, moves them, combines them, and so on, during the critical-thinking session. It's a good idea to change secretaries at least once during a lengthy session. Secretaries should use symbols and drawings occasionally, to save time, and liven up the session, and provide visual stimulation.

Storyboarding Materials. Originally, story boards consisted of cork wall boards covering the entire sides of several walls; note cards were tacked to this surface. Thus, in addition to a facilitator and a secretary, a tacker was also needed. Later, people began to use scotch tape to attach the cards to any wall; this procedure required a taper. Now most story boards are created on writing surfaces such as a series of chalkboards or a series of white boards. On these it is easy to add, delete, or move ideas. I prefer to use white boards and different-colored markers to differentiate the topic header, the headers, the subbers, and the siders. You can also use different colors to distinguish each column from the rest. If you use note cards, the topic card should be 8" x 10", the headers and subbers 4" x 6". Depending on which system you use, be it pushpin cards, taped cards, Post It Notes, erasable wall boards or chalkboards, you'll need push pins, scissors, wide marking pens for paper or boards, chalk, and a supply of cards or Post It Notes. A Polaroid camera comes in handy for taking pictures of completed boards.

Another Example

Let's say that your creative problem-solving project is to improve productivity. The topic card would read "Improve Productivity." Then your project team would consider what they needed to do to talk about, or think about regarding this problem.

Some major considerations that might arise, to be written up on header cards, are the following: Purpose, Productivity Defined, Good Examples, Causes of High Productivity, Causes of Low Productivity, Educational Theories and Resources, Major Methods, Implementation Concepts, and Miscellaneous. Remember always to have a header labeled "Purpose" and one labeled "Miscellaneous," and to complete the purpose header before brainstorming the other headers. Next work with each header in depth to develop the subbers under it.

Miscellaneous: At first we had only "background" as a subber on our story board about storyboarding. Now, in Figure 5.7, three more subbers have been added. Visual - One of the most important characteristics of storyboarding is its visuality. Not just the artwork which may be added, but the very fact that the words are listed so that everyone can see them and respond to them. Flexible - One reason I like this process is that it is so flexible. You don't have to follow the rules exactly. You can change the boards around easily. Symbols - The use of symbols makes it easier to be creative, be-

101
CREATIVE
PROBLEM
SOLVING
TECHNIQUES

173

cause of their visuality, and because they more quickly summarize concepts than do words.

The Personal Story Board

The personal story board is a form that you can use to copy information from a wall story board. It can be carried conveniently in a briefcase. It will come in handy if you want to work on a project when you're away from your story board wall. Figure 5.8 shows a sample personal story board form.

Suggestions for Putting Storyboarding to Work

1. To start, choose the walls you'll devote to storyboarding and acquire the necessary materials.
2. Choose your first topic or objective.
3. Organize your project team. Notify the team members of the topic and type of story board.
4. Choose a facilitator, writer, and pinner/taper, and initiate the first creative-thinking session. Review ground rules. Do something to warm up the participants and get them excited about the project.
5. After a break, then, hold a critical-thinking session to evaluate the ideas generated in the creative-thinking session. Begin by reviewing ground rules. Reorganize your story board as you proceed.
6. Follow up your planning board with an ideas story board. Then use an organization story board and, if necessary, a communications board or some version thereof.

Experiences with Storyboarding

Storyboarding is not nearly as well known or as frequently utilized as brainstorming, yet for more complex problems, it is the best process to use. For example, a data transactions company that was seeking to become more innovative used storyboarding to develop a management structure that encouraged and systematically approved of innovative projects.

The process has been used successfully for a wide range of complex issues, from helping solve quality problems in the

Figure 5.8 Personal Story Board

Personal Story Board

Date ______________ Topic ______________

Header	Header	Header	Header	Header	Header	Header
Subber	Subber	Subber	Subber	Subber	Subber	Subber
____	____	____	____	____	____	____
____	____	____	____	____	____	____
____	____	____	____	____	____	____
____	____	____	____	____	____	____
____	____	____	____	____	____	____
____	____	____	____	____	____	____
____	____	____	____	____	____	____
____	____	____	____	____	____	____
____	____	____	____	____	____	____
____	____	____	____	____	____	____
____	____	____	____	____	____	____
____	____	____	____	____	____	____

health care industry at West Paces Ferry Hospital in Atlanta, Georgia,[59] to information system project design and implementation,[60] to writing technical proposals.[61] It is a major part of Frito-Lay's creative problem-solving program.[62]

Noack and Dean Insurance Agency of Sacramento, California uses story boards as the focal point for its planning center.[63] Rockwell Hanford Operations of Richland, Virginia, used both brainstorming and storyboarding to formulate its information resource management plan (IRM), under which the business and scientific functions were merged into a single information system.[64]

Final Observations on Storyboarding

The beauty of this technique is that it is flexible and readily adaptable to your needs. If you don't like the exact system, change it a little to meet your requirements. When you begin using the process, keep it simple. As you become comfortable with the system you can expand your applications of it. However, you may need to spread story boards over several days to maintain the group's energy levels, and several boards may be necessary to solve very complex problems. Personally, I believe it is the best group problem-solving technique for complex problems.

SUMMARY OF STEPS

1. A group consisting of eight to twelve people, a leader, and a recorder are selected.
2. The problem is defined and identified as the topic header at the top of the story board.
3. The purpose and miscellaneous headers are written down. The purpose header is brainstormed.
4. The other headers are identified through brainstorming.
5. Each header's subtopics are identified through brainstorming.
6. After a break, the critical session occurs, using different rules from those used in the creative session.
7. Ideas, communication, and organization story boards follow, using the same steps.

94/30. SYNECTICS

Synectics is a form of group brainstorming that relies heavily on analogies and metaphors, association, and the excursion technique to help the imagination find relationships between seemingly unrelated objects, ideas, products, persons, and so on.[65] The dual purpose of this process is to learn (i.e., make the strange familiar) and to innovate (i.e., make the familiar strange).[66] The process usually uses seven people: a problem owner, a facilitator, and five other members.

According to its creator, William J.J. Gordon, synectics is based on three key assumptions:

1. Creativity is latent to some degree in everyone.
2. Creativity is more closely related to the emotional and nonrational than to the intellectual and rational.
3. These emotional elements can be harnessed through training and practice.[67]

Three mechanisms are used to facilitate such behavior:[68]

1. Direct analogy — finding out how the object is like other things that you are familiar with, such as biological systems.
2. Personal analogy — pretending you are the object of your study. This is role playing in its broadest sense.
3. Symbolic analogy — developing a compressed expression of the problem at hand—a key word. Then one or two analogies related to this are used to brainstorm.

One of the major differences between synectics and normal brainstorming is the addition of criticism to the process. In fact, participants are encouraged to criticize, even to be sarcastic, but only at the right time. (As some versions of the criticism process can be quite harsh, the leader's role is made more difficult by this step.) These sessions can be highly charged emotionally. Synectics seeks to harness the criticism and what feelings it evokes.[69]

At any step in the process the facilitator may interject the use of free association, analogies and metaphors, or the excursion technique. I have found that if you focus on these

101
CREATIVE
PROBLEM
SOLVING
TECHNIQUES

177

aspects of the process, profitable results may emerge. It is the use of these processes and criticism that distinguishes synectics from brainstorming.[70]

SUMMARY OF STEPS

1. The problem is identified. The owner of the problem defines it, beginning with "How to ..."
2. The problem is analyzed briefly. The owner of the problem describes why it is a problem, what solutions have been attempted, and the objectives for the session.
3. Goals and wishes are stated. Participants write down personal goals and wishes for the problem. These are the vague, often "wild and crazy" beginnings of solutions.
4. Group goals and wishes are listed. Once individuals have completed their lists of goals and wishes, these are listed by the facilitator on a board. A round-robin approach such as is used with the nominal group technique works well.
5. The problem owner attempts to identify a possible solution.
6. The problem owner lists three strengths and three weaknesses of the possible solution.
7. The group critiques the proposed solution.

95/31. TAKE FIVE

"Take five" is a game that goes beyond brainstorming in its use of the small group.[71] The game takes about forty minutes. "Take five" lends itself to all sorts of problem solving, from strategic planning and forecasting to construction of questionnaires.

SUMMARY OF STEPS

1. A topic is selected.
2. The leader describes it to the participants and clarifies issues if necessary.
3. Participants spend two minutes preparing lists of ideas related to the topic.
4. Dividing into teams of five, they pool their ideas to produce longer lists of items, which they rank in order of importance.
5. All the groups, meeting together, create a short list composed of the most important items from each group, limiting the total to ten.
6. These items are discussed and assessed.

96/32. TKJ METHOD

Developed in 1964, the KJ (Kawakita Jiro) method is named for its originator, Jiro Kawakita, then professor of anthropology at the Tokyo Institute of Technology.[72] The original "kami-kire ho" or "scrap paper method" was used to generate new conceptual images from raw data. In its later stages, this technique is highly visual and helps link verbal concepts with visual representations. The TKJ method builds on the KJ method and provides more steps for defining the problem. There are two parts to the TKJ process: problem definition and problem solution.

SUMMARY OF STEPS

I. Problem Definition

1. Participants are given a central theme and asked to write as many ideas about the problem as possible on 3 x 5 cards (which have replaced the original pieces of scrap paper). Ideas must be stated briefly. The point of this step is for each individual to think of as many perspectives on the problem as possible. Each participant can generate fifteen to twenty ideas in a five- to ten-minute time span.

2. The cards are collected and consensually sorted into very general categories. To accomplish this, the leader collects the cards and redistributes them so that no person has his or her own cards. TKJ encourages the use of humor in sorting the cards and discussing the ideas.

3. The leader reads one of the cards aloud.

4. Participants find cards in their stacks that contain related ideas and read these aloud. Alternatively, the leader can stack the cards as they are collected without having them read aloud. A collection of cards, which constitute a set of thoughts, is built in this way.

5. The group gives each set of cards a name that captures the essence of the thoughts represented, that is, the essence of the problem.

6. The process continues until all cards are in named sets.

7. The named sets are combined into an all-inclusive group that is named the way the other sets were. This final set represents a consensus definition of the problem. The purpose of sorting the ideas into groups is to bring new ways of thinking to old categories of issues.

Continued

II. Problem Solution

1. Participants write down possible solutions to the problem on 3 x 5 cards. These ideas may or may not be related to any that have preceded.
2. The leader collects the cards and redistributes them as in part I. The leader then reads one idea aloud. As before, participants find cards that are related to it. These are read aloud and a named solution set emerges.
3. As before, all cards are eventually placed in named solution sets.
4. As before, an all-inclusive solution set is derived and named.

Variations: Rather than following Step 7 of Part I Problem Definition and combining sets into one overall definition, I like to use Step II for each of the named sets identified in Step 6 of Part I. I find this gives us a better handle on the problem than recombining. This approach makes TKJ similar to the storyboarding technique.

A graphical representation of the group's ideas may emerge as the leader/recorder, when soliciting the ideas, draws a conceptual picture of them on a writing surface in front of the group. New ideas are then generated and written down by participants. These may be derived from the conceptual picture itself or from a discussion of it. Eventually these ideas may also be shared.

Like many of the Japanese creativity techniques, the TKJ method, which is extremely popular in Japan, uses cards, visual maps, and association of thoughts to generate new ideas. Some U.S. participants feel that it is too complicated and that it restricts creativity. Others like the fact that it guarantees anonymity.

A FINAL NOTE

Thirty-two techniques are described in this chapter. You may find five to ten that you feel comfortable with. But try them all, and revisit them all occasionally to avoid getting in a rut.

REFERENCES

[0] James M. Higgins, *The Management Challenge*, 2nd ed., (New York: Macmillan, 1994), Chapters 1 and 15.

[1] Ibid., p. 133.

[2] Ibid.

[3] David J. Placek, "Creativity Survey Shows Who's Doing What; How to Get Your Team on the Road to Creativity," *Marketing News* (November 6, 1989), p. 14.

[4] Alex Osborn, *Applied Imagination* (New York: Charles Scribner & Sons, 1953), pp. 297-304; also see, Robert Kerwin, "Brainstorming as a Flexible Management Tool," *Personnel Journal* (May 1983), pp. 414-418.

[5] "Group Techniques: Part 2, Alternatives to Brainstorming," *Small Business Report* (October 1981), p. 15.

[6] "IP Offers Creative Partnership," *Purchasing World* (August 1990), pp. 38–41.

[7] Edward D. Cohen and Robert H. Knospe, "Professional Excellence Committee Benefits Technical Professionals at DuPont," *Research-Technology Management* (July/August, 1990), pp. 46-50.

[8] "Federal Express: Employees Eliminate Problems Instead of Fighting Fires," *Business Marketing* (February 1990), pp. 40, 42.

[9] Carol Kennedy, "The Transformation of AT&T," *Long Range Planning* (June 1989), pp. 10-17.

[10] The author was the leader of these sessions.

[11] N.A. Howard, "Creativity: A Special Report," *Success*, p. 56.

[12] Karen Lowry Miller, "55 Miles Per Gallon: How Honda Did It," *Business Week* (September 23, 1991), pp. 82, 83.

[13] This discussion of Japanese creativity techniques and of the four techniques discussed later in the chapter are taken from: Sheridan M. Tatsuno, *Created in Japan: From Imitators to World-Class Innovators*, (New York: Harper & Row, Ballenger Division, 1990), pp. 104-115; and a summary of these as discussed in Sheridan M. Tatsuno, "Creating Breakthroughs the Japanese Way," *R&D Magazine* (February 1990), pp. 137-142.

[14] Arthur B. VanGundy, *Creative Problem Solving* (New York: Quorum Books, 1987), pp. 131–144.

[15] Ibid.

[16] Horst Greschka, "Perspectives on Using Various Creativity Techniques," in Stanley S. Gryskiewicz, *Creativity Week II, 1979 Proceedings* (Greensboro, North Carolina: Center for Creative Leadership, 1979) pp. 51-55.

[17] Lea Hall, "Can you Picture That?" *Training & Development Journal* (September 1990), pp. 79-81.

[18] Richard Bandler and John Grinder, *Frogs Into Princes: Neurolinguistic Programming* (Moab, UT: Real People Press, 1979).

[19] James F. Bandrowski, "Taking Creative Leaps," *Planning Review* (January/February 1990), pp. 34-38.

[20] Sheridan M. Tatsuno, "Creating Breakthroughs, the Japanese Way," *R&D* (February, 1990), pp. 136-142; Simon Majaro, *The Creative Gap: Managing Ideas for Profit*, (London: Longman, 1988), pp. 106-119.

101
CREATIVE
PROBLEM
SOLVING
TECHNIQUES

181
n

[21] Most of this discussion is taken from Janet Fiero, "The Crawford Slip Method," *Quality Progress* (May 1992), pp. 40–43; also see, Robert M. Krone, "Improving Brainpower Productivity," *Journal for Quality and Participation* (December 1990), pp. 80-84.

[22] Ray Dull, "Delphi Forecasting: Market Research Method of the 1990s," *Marketing News* (August 29, 1988), p. 17.

[23] J. Daniel Couger, "Key Human Resource Issues in IS in the 1990s: Interviews of IS Executives Versus Human Resource Executives," *Information and Management* (April 1988), pp 161-174.

[24] James F. Robeson, "The Future of Business Logistics: A Delphi Study Predicting Future Trends in Business Logistics," *Journal of Business Logistics* (#2, 1988), pp. 1-14.

[25] Yeong Wee Yong, Kau Ah Keng, Tan Leng Leng, "A Delphi Forecast for the Singapore Tourism Industry: Future Scenario and Marketing Implications," *European Journal of Marketing* (November 1989), pp. 15-26.

[26] Magaly Olivero, "Get Crazy! How to Have a Break Through Idea," *Working Woman* (September 1990), p. 144.

[27] As reported in Stan S. Gryskiewicz and J.T. Shields, "Issues and Observations," (Greenville, N.C.: Center for Creative Leadership) (November 1983), p. 5.

[28] Horst Geschka, loc. cit.

[29] Ibid.

[30] Arthur B. VanGundy, Creative Problem Solving (New York: Quorum, 1987), pp. 136.

[31] Terry L. Campbell, "Technology Update: Group Decision Support Systems," *Journal of Accountancy* (July 1990), pp. 47-50.

[32] Presentation by Ron Remillard of Wilson Learning Corporation to Central Florida Chapter of American Society for Training & Development (Orlando, Florida, February 17, 1987).

[33] Joseph S. Cavarretta, "Computer-Aided Decisions," *Association Management* (December 1992), pp. 12–13; Wayne Eckerson, "Users Enthused About Electronic Meetings," *Network World* (June 15, 1992), p. 43; Paul Saffo, "Same Time, Same Place: Groupware," *Personal Computing* (March 20, 1990), pp. 57-58; Julie Barker, "The State of the Art for Decision Making," *Successful Meetings* (November 1989), pp. 51-53.

[34] Edward Glasman, "Creative Problem Solving", *Supervisory Management*, (March 1989) pp. 17-18.

[35] Bryan W. Mattimore, "Brainstormer's Boot Camp," *Success* (October 1991), p. 24.

[36] John Case, "Customer Service: The Last Word," *Inc.* (April 1991), pp. 89-93.

[37] Knut Holt, "Consulting in Innovation through Intercompany Study Groups," *Technovation* (July 1990), pp. 347-353

[38] Robert Bookman, "Rousing the Creative Spirit," *Training & Development Journal* (November 1988), pp. 67–71.

[39] Sheridan M. Tatsuno, *Created in Japan*, op. cit., pp. 110-113.

[40] Sheridan M. Tatsuno, *Created in Japan*, op. cit., pp. 109-110.

[41] Carl E. Gregory, *The Management of Intelligence* (New York: McGraw-Hill, 1967), pp. 200–202.

[42] Sheridan M. Tatsuno, *Created in Japan*, op. cit., p. 110.

[43] Andre L. Delbecq, Andrew H. Van de Ven, and D.H. Gustafson, *Group Techniques for Program Planning* (Glenview, Ill.: Scott Foresman & Company, 1975).

[44] Don Hellriegel, John W. Slocum, Richard W. Woodman, *Organizational Behavior*, 4th ed. (St. Paul, Minnesota: West Publishing Company, 1986) p. 259.

[45] See S. Scott Sink, "Using the Nominal Group Technique Effectively," *National Productivity Review*, (Spring 1983) p. 181.

[46] Aubrey L. Mendelow and S. Jay Liebowitz, "Difficulties in Making OD a Part of Organizational Strategy," *Human Resource Planning* (1989, #4), pp. 317–329.

[47] James B. Thomas, Reuben R. McDaniel, Jr., and Michael J. Dooris, "Strategic Issue Analysis: NGT + Decision Analysis for Resolving Strategic Issues," *Journal of Applied Behavioral Science* (1989), #2, pp. 189-200.

[48] Edward J. Szewczak, "Building a Strategic Data Base," *Long Range Planning* (April 1988), pp. 97-103.

[49] "Incentive Magazine: Nominal Groups in Action," *Incentive* (November 1988, pp. 60–62.

[50] William M. Fox, "'Anonymity and Other Keys to Successful Problem Solving Meetings," *National Productivity Review* (Spring 1989), pp. 145-156; William M. Fox, "The Improved Nominal Group Technique (INGT)," *Journal of Management Development* (1989), #1, pp. 20-27.

[51] "Group Techniques: Part 2, Alternatives to Brainstorming," *Small Business Report* (October 1981), pp. 15-17.

[52] Bryan W. Mattimore, loc. cit.

[53] Horst Geschka, loc. cit.

[54] Paul J. H. Schoemaker and Cornelius A. J. M. van der Heijden, "Integrating Scenarios Into Strategic Planning at Royal Dutch Shell," *Planning Review* (May-June 1992), pp. 41–46.

[55] Simon Majaro, *The Creative Gap* (Great Britain: Longman, 1988) pp. 202-203.

[56] Fred Mobasheri, Lowell H. Orren and Fereidoon P. Sioshansi, "Scenario Planning at Southern California Edison," *Interfaces* (September-October 1989), pp. 31–44.

[57] Horst Geschka, loc. cit.

[58] Mike Vance, "Storyboarding" from "Creativity " a series of audio cassette tapes on creativity, taken from the accompanying booklet to the tape series (Chicago: Nightengale-Conant, 1982); Jerry McNellis, "An Experience in Creative Thinking," (New Brighton, PA: The McNellis Company, no date); and Lawrence F. Lottier, Jr., "Storyboarding Your Way to Successful Training, *Public Personnel Management* (Winter 1986), pp. 421-427.

[59] Lawrence F. Lottier, Jr., ibid.

[60] Janis M. Czuszak and Albert L. Lederer, "On Time and Within Budget," *Data Management*, March 1987, pp. 34-38.

[61] Robert A. Barakat, "Storyboarding Can Help Your Proposal," *IEEE Transactions on Professional Communication*, March 1989, pp. 20-25.

[62] As described to the author by a Frito-Lay staff member.

[63] Kenneth B. Noack, "Striving for Agency Excellence," *American Agent & Broker*, January 1991, pp. 59-62.

[64] Darrell S. Corbin, "Bottom-Up IRM Planning: How it Worked at Rockwell," *Information Strategy: The Executive's Journal*, Fall, 1986, pp. 4-11.

[65] Morris I. Stein, *Stimulating Creativity: Group Procedures*, (New York: Academic Press, 1975), Chapter XV, pp. 172-221; William J.J. Gordon, *Synectics: The Development of Creative Capacity*, (New York: Collier Macmillan, 1961).

[66] William J.J. Gordon and George M. Prince, *The Operational Mechanisms of Synectics*, (Cambridge, Mass.: Synectics Incorporated, 1960), p. 2.

[67] Tom Alexander, "Synectics: Inventing by the Madness Method," *Fortune* (August 1965), p. 168.

[68] R. A. Proctor, "The Use of Metaphors to Aid the Process of Creative Problem Solving," *Personnel Review* (1989), #4, pp. 33-42.

[69] Gordon and Prince, pp. 6-12.

[70] Ibid. For a somewhat different version see: Morris I. Stein, *Stimulating Creativity: Volume 2, Group Procedures* (New York: Academic Press, 1975), pp. 196–202.

[71] Sivasailam Thiagarajan, "Take Five for Better Brainstorming," *Training & Development Journal* (February 1991), pp. 37-42.

[72] Sheridan M. Tatsuno, *Created in Japan*, op. cit., pp. 104-106 for the KJ method; Michael Michalko, *Thinkertoys: A Handbook of Business Creativity for the 90s* (Berkeley, CA: Ten Speed Press, 1991) pp. 308–311 for the TJK method.

CHAPTER 6

Techniques for
Choosing
Among
Alternatives

•

Techniques for
Implementation

•

Additional
Advice on
Implementation

•

Control

CREATIVE TECHNIQUES
FOR
CHOOSING AMONG ALTERNATIVES,
IMPLEMENTATION, AND CONTROL

You're going to take funds from my superbly managed division to start
that harebrained scheme?

> — Richard Foster
> Senior partner, McKinsey & Co.,
> commenting on the politics of selling innovations in organizations.
> This represents a typical manager's reaction to a new idea
> in someone else's department.

101
CREATIVE
PROBLEM
SOLVING
TECHNIQUES

185

CHOOSING AMONG ALTERNATIVES

Choosing among alternatives is usually described as a rational process. Criteria were selected earlier, in the identification stage of the creative problem-solving process. Now the various alternatives that have been generated must be compared to those criteria and a choice must be made. (See Figure 2.2.)

Screening of ideas is carried out in two stages. In the first stage, an idea is screened for level of creativity and degree of compatibility with organizational objectives and constraints. In the second stage, the idea is screened for its potential impact. For product innovations, this would require a market analysis. For process, marketing, and management innovations, this

THE
VERIFIER

USELESS   VALID

would require examining the impact on the organization it-self, and possibly potential market benefits such as being able to reduce prices because of lower costs.

This chapter reviews two creative techniques designed spe-cifically for use in comparing criteria to alternatives: the screening matrix for ideas and dot voting.

97/1. THE SCREENING MATRIX FOR IDEAS

Innovation consultant Simon Majaro has developed a screen-ing matrix for ideas, an excellent way of choosing ideas that will pass the first hurdle.[1] Figure 6.1 is an example of such a matrix. Each axis represents summary criteria. The creativ-ity axis represents idea attractiveness, which might include such qualities as originality and perceived value. The inno-vation axis represents the idea's compatibility with organi-zational objectives and constraints.[2] This might include such issues as availability of financial and human resources.

Figure 6.1 Screening Matrix for Ideas

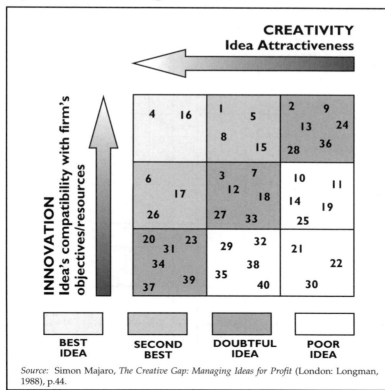

Source: Simon Majaro, *The Creative Gap: Managing Ideas for Profit* (London: Longman, 1988), p.44.

101
CREATIVE
PROBLEM
SOLVING
TECHNIQUES

187

In Figure 6.1 forty ideas have been rated as high, medium, or low in creativity and high, medium, or low in innovation. The intersection of those evaluations is indicated by the idea number. For example, idea number 30 was evaluated low in both creativity and innovation. Similarly, idea number 6 was rated high in creativity and medium in innovation. This figure represents an elementary screening matrix in that an idea's position is based on an individual's estimates using the simple descriptive terms of <u>high</u>, <u>medium</u> and <u>low</u>.

To provide more accurate judgments, the idea's position in the matrix can be based on more specific criteria and an evaluation of their relevance to the situation. Such criteria are presented in

Figure 6.2 Complex Screening Matrix for Ideas

Criteria of Evaluation (Examples only)	Weight	10	9	8	7	6	5	4	3	2	1	0	Score
A					**B**								**AxB**
Idea Attractiveness													
Ease of implementation	0.10												
Originality	0.15												
Protectable/sustainable	0.10												
User-friendly	0.10												
Global Acceptability	0.05												
Compatibility Criteria													
Available finance	0.20												
Provision of solution to specific problem	0.10												
Our image	0.05												
Our ability to protect (e.g. patent)	0.05												
Our marketing competence	0.10												
	1.00								Total score				

Source: Simon Majaro, *The Creative Gap: Managing Ideas for Profit* (London: Longman, 1988), p.49.

Figure 6.3

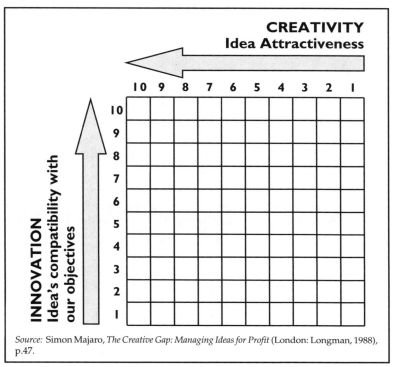

Source: Simon Majaro, *The Creative Gap: Managing Ideas for Profit* (London: Longman, 1988), p.47.

Table 6.1. The relative values of an idea could be calculated using Figure 6.2. The idea would then be placed on a matrix like the one portrayed in Figure 6.3.

The second stage of the screening process can also be accomplished using a screening matrix. For a product innovation, the two axes would be the company's potential strengths (relative to this particular innovation) and the idea's market potential. Using a standard General Electric portfolio matrix approach, more specific criteria are identified in Table 6.2.[3] A process identical to that used in Figure 6.2 would result in the placement of the idea on a matrix similar to Figure 6.3.

SUMMARY OF STEPS

1. Create a standard four-cell matrix in which one axis represents creativity and the other innovation.
2. Ideas are placed on the matrix according to how well they meet established criteria as defined by the axes.

TABLE 6.1 Criteria for Idea Evaluation

Criteria of Attractiveness	Criteria of Compatibility
(Examples Only)	*(Examples Only)*
Originality	Compatibility with:
Simplicity	Available financial resources
User friendly	Available human resources
Easy to implement	Corporate image
Elegant	Ability to protect (e.g., patent)
Difficult to copy	Need to solve problem

Source: Simon Majaro, *The Creative Gap: Managing Ideas for Profit* (London: Longman, 1988), p. 46.

TABLE 6.2 Criteria for Business Unit Evaluation

Product Strength/ Competitive Position	Market Potential
(Examples Only)	*(Examples Only)*
Size	Size
Growth	Market growth, pricing
Share	Market diversity
Position	Competitive structure
Profitability	Industry profitability
Margin	Technical rate
Technology position	Social factors
Image	Environmental factors
Pollution	Legal factors
People	Human factors

Source: Figure from *Strategic Management: Text and Cases*, Fifth ed. by James M. Higgins and Julian W. Vincze, copyright © 1993 by Harcourt Brace & Company, reproduced by permission of the publisher.

98/2. DOT VOTING

Many standard ways of making choices involve voting. There are also some creative ways such as the nominal group technique. Another creative way of choosing among alternatives is dot voting. The ideas are written on a large surface such as a poster board, flip chart or white board. Participants then indicate their choices with stick-on dots.[4] Participants may have only one vote or more than one. They may or may not be allowed to vote for their own ideas.[5]

IMPLEMENTATION

Having an idea is not enough. Specific action plans for bringing the innovation to the market, or for incorporating the innovation into the organizational process must be determined. Resources must be obtained to complete these action plans. Often, other members of the organization must be convinced of the merits of that idea. Selling an idea requires different behavior than creating one. You must master both creative and selling processes if your idea is to reach fruition. Implementation therefore is largely a matter of working within the organization's culture. This chapter examines creativity techniques designed to help the manager within that context.

99/1. HOW-HOW DIAGRAM

The how-how diagram is similar to the why-why diagram described in Chapter 3.[6] It seeks to identify the steps necessary to implement a solution. Instead of asking "Why?" the problem solver(s) ask "How?" The agreed-upon solution is stated on the left side of a piece of paper, with more detailed action plans placed on the right in a decision tree format. (See Figure 6.4 for an abbreviated how-how diagram.) Each time a solution is listed, the question "How?" is asked. Problem solvers answer with a more detailed action plan.

**HOW?
HOW?**

Using the problem suggested in Chapter 3 for the why-why diagram as an example, the first solution mentioned is "improve product." Asking "how" results in four principal ways of improving the product: "improve packaging, improve product quality, lengthen shelf

101
CREATIVE
PROBLEM
SOLVING
TECHNIQUES

191

Figure 6.4 The How-How Diagram

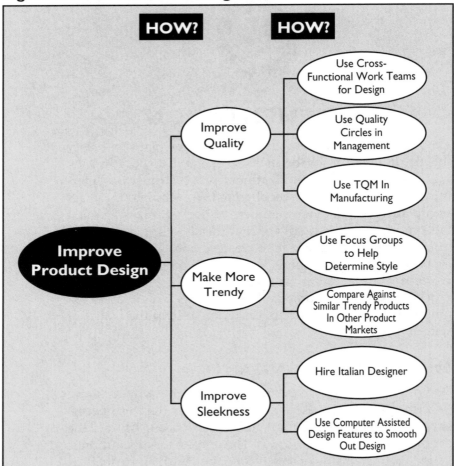

life, and shorten delivery time." For each of these the question "how" is asked, resulting in more detailed actions for each. For example, the second-level solution of improving quality consists of three more detailed actions: use cross-functional work teams during design, use quality circles for manufacturing, use TQM in manufacturing. Once a diagram has been completed, the final details for all implementation plans may be agreed upon.

This is an excellent technique for forcing problem solvers to think about the details of implementation.

1. The agreed-upon solution to a problem is placed on the left side of a piece of paper.
2. A decision tree of more detailed action plans obtained by asking "How?" at each stage of the process is formed to the right of the solution.
3. Beginning with the first solution, each time a solution is listed, the question "How?" is asked. The responses are recorded on branches of the decision tree.
4. The question "How?" is asked again. This results in additional branches on the decision tree.
5. The process continues until sufficiently detailed implementation plans have been established.

100/2. BE A WARRIOR WHEN SELLING YOUR IDEAS

Roger von Oech, a noted creativity consultant and author, suggests that there are four distinct roles that must be filled during the creativity/innovation process: explorer, artist, judge, and warrior.[7]

"When you're searching for new information, be an **EXPLORER.**

When you're turning your resources into new ideas, be an **ARTIST.**

When you're evaluating the merits of an idea, be a **JUDGE.**

When you're carrying your idea into action, be a **WARRIOR.**"[8]

101
CREATIVE
PROBLEM
SOLVING
TECHNIQUES

193

Our interest in this chapter is in the warrior role. The other roles were discussed in other chapters, although under different names and in different contexts. For example, in terms of the creative problem-solving model presented in Chapter 2, the explorer and the artist are active in analyzing the environment, recognizing a problem, identifying a problem, and generating alternatives, with the artist primarily responsible for generating alternatives. The judge is active in making assumptions and making a choice. The warrior would be active in making a choice and in implementing the creative result in the sense of getting the organization to adopt it and transform it into an innovation.

Often a person who can be an explorer and artist finds it difficult to be a judge or a warrior. Even people who can assume the first three roles often find it difficult to be a warrior. That is why many firms separate these functions, normally combining the first two in the role of the creator, and asking a group, usually made up of professional staff or managers but sometimes a creativity circle, to judge the value of the creative result. Then a manager or professional staff person may serve as the product champion, moving the product through the various stages of the approval process within the firm.[9]

Von Oech observes that the individual must move from one role to another and that this movement is difficult for many people. If you are not able to change roles readily, you must either force yourself to assume roles in which you are uncomfortable or find yourself a champion. Whether you pursue the role of warrior yourself or find a champion, the selling part of the process must be accomplished.

101/3. FORCE-FIELD ANALYSIS

Organizational development is but one type of change management. Regardless of which program is used to manage change, the manager making the changes will invariably be faced with resistance. To better manage change, the problem solver needs to understand force-field analysis, a concept developed by Kurt Lewin, a pioneer in the study of change. Lewin suggests that change results from the rela-

Figure 6.5 Force-Field Analysis

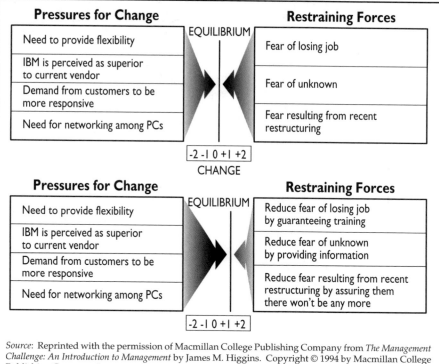

Pressures for Change   **Restraining Forces**

EQUILIBRIUM

Need to provide flexibility	Fear of losing job
IBM is perceived as superior to current vendor	Fear of unknown
Demand from customers to be more responsive	
Need for networking among PCs	Fear resulting from recent restructuring

-2 -1 0 +1 +2
CHANGE

Pressures for Change   **Restraining Forces**

EQUILIBRIUM

Need to provide flexibility	Reduce fear of losing job by guaranteeing training
IBM is perceived as superior to current vendor	Reduce fear of unknown by providing information
Demand from customers to be more responsive	
Need for networking among PCs	Reduce fear resulting from recent restructuring by assuring them there won't be any more

-2 -1 0 +1 +2

Source: Reprinted with the permission of Macmillan College Publishing Company from *The Management Challenge: An Introduction to Management* by James M. Higgins. Copyright © 1994 by Macmillan College Publishing Company, Inc.

tive strengths of competing driving and restraining forces.[10] The driving forces push the organization toward change; the restraining forces push against change. The actual change that emerges is a consequence of the interaction of the two sets of forces. If you want change, you should push. But the natural tendency of those you are pushing is to resist the change, to push back. According to Lewin, the driving forces activate the restraining forces. He suggests that decreasing the restraining forces is a more effective way of encouraging change than increasing the driving forces.

Figure 6.5 portrays the use of force-field analysis to reduce resistance to a change from using a single computer vendor, UNISYS, to using multiple computer vendors—IBM, Digital Equipment Company (DEC), and UNISYS—for the information division of a major entertainment company. This is a partial analysis of the situation as viewed by that division's managers.[11] As you can see, the managers determined that

101
CREATIVE
PROBLEM
SOLVING
TECHNIQUES

195

Figure 6.6 Selling Others on Your Creative Ideas

	SELLING OTHERS ON				
Purpose	**Preparation**	**Who**	**How**	**Ability/ Personality**	**Style**
To effectively sell an idea.	Convince self first.	Peers. Boss.	Stress benefits.	Competitive/ comfortable.	Presentation skills.
To make myself more successful.	Provide examples of usefulness.	Subordinates. Power bases.	Know needs. Show profits.	Visualize/ enthusiasm. Learn from perseverance.	Know yourself. Know audience.
To make more money for company.	Know obstacles and prepare to overcome.	Clients. Leaders.	Help reduce costs.	Cope with failure.	Keep it in perspective.
To make more income for myself.	Gather supportive facts.			Probes.	
To make job easier.	Seek support.				
	Find coalition power base.				
	Know politics of situation.				
	Be able to use tools/ presentation skills.				
	Bracing people — drop hints.				

YOUR CREATIVE IDEAS

Credibility	Costs	Culture	Results	Presentation Skills	Personality	Misc.
How to raise current level.	How much.	Innovative or not.	Long term vs. short term.	Factual.	Innovator vs. adaptor.	
Use credible descriptions.	How financed.	Receptive to creativity or not.	Quantifiable.	Big picture.	Believe in idea yourself.	
Use information to support.		Who are decision makers.	Qualitative.	Persuasive.	Persistence.	
			How will this fit into strategic plan?	Learnable.	Self-assurance.	
		How do you get to them: — politics.		Pizzazz.		
				Know yourself.		
		Two-stage sales process.				

101
CREATIVE
PROBLEM
SOLVING
TECHNIQUES

197

the best way to move toward the change was to reduce employee fears by providing job guarantees and training, and to provide more open communication.

ADDITIONAL ADVICE ON IMPLEMENTATION

Figure 6.6 is a story board created by a group of twenty upper- and middle-level managers from a cross section of firms, industries, and functional specialties. This story board indicates the key issues in making a sale, that is, being an effective champion of your creative ideas. Add to it or create your own.

The Innovative Edge in Action 6.1, on the politics of innovation, does not describe a creativity technique per se. However, it provides some guidance that can be used creatively. A typical idea approval situation is described in The Innovative Edge in Action 6.2.

THE POLITICS OF INNOVATION

For all their vows to reform, somehow managers keep coming up with ways to stifle new ideas.

See the top executives. See them sit in a circle, on the moonlit sands of Lyford Cay, in the bosky groves of the Greenbrier, whispering to one another. See them beat their naked chests, their hands still dripping with the gore of restructuring. Hear their guttural chant: *in*-no-va-tion, *in*-no-va-tion.

Yes, connoisseurs of trendy corporate-speak, a new buzzword is emerging. By now just about everybody has restructured, paring down to those so-called core businesses. Nasty surprise: Many of these residual enterprises are growing at a mere 1 percent or 2 percent a year. Acquisitions, anyone? No, no, no, the experts inveigh, that's how you got in trouble last time around. So how is a self-respecting company supposed to grow? The increasingly popular answer: new products, new services, new ways to achieve higher quality at lower cost. In short, innovation.

"Most people give it lip service," says Glenda Keller, a consultant with Synectics, a Cambridge, Massachusetts, firm that helps companies tackle the problem of innovation. Indeed, Keller argues, "it would be suicide these days not to." The stock market is watching. But to go beyond uttering the latest pieties, to actually do something, ah, there the going gets rough.

Deep thinkers on the subject distinguish invention, coming up with a new idea, from innovation, shepherding that idea through the toils of the organization so that it eventually emerges as a new product or procedure. Invention, at least commercial grade, is surprisingly easy, the experts find. Consultant Thomas D. Kuczmarski, author of *Managing New Products*, asserts that "if you and I sat down and brainstormed about a business for a couple of hours, we could come up with maybe twenty ideas for new products." A few would probably be worth pursuing. But just try it at your average organization.

CONTINUES ON PAGE 200

THE POLITICS OF INNOVATION

Continued from page 199

The problem, all too often, is politics, defined in this case as the competition within a company for limited corporate resources—money, power, or opportunities for promotion. "One man's innovation is another man's failure," notes McKinsey consultant Richard Foster, author of the 1986 book *Innovation: The Attacker's Advantage* Foster notes how managers think, "You're going to take funds from my superbly managed division to start *that* harebrained scheme?"

Veterans of the corporate wars are already wearily familiar with a few innovation-derailing patterns of behavior: the not-invented-here syndrome, the tendency to fight over turf, the rush to gun down any wild geese who challenge the system. What folks who have been pushing corporate innovation for the past few years have discovered is that organizations, and their denizens, have even more ways of resisting change. Some are carefully crafted political stratagems, others seemingly automatic responses of the corporate nervous system. Some examples:

•**The dummy task force.** Top management sets up a group to spearhead new product development. But, as Synectic's Keller observes, the brass betray their underlying lack of commitment by not assigning the task force any concrete goals, or failing to set a definite beginning,

middle, and end to the effort. Or the higher-ups use the group as a place to park good company soldiers who are temporarily out of a job, but whom the company doesn't want to lose. Over time, the big boys' attention shifts elsewhere, and whatever the supposedly special team ends up recommending somehow gets lost.

•**The task force as a setup.** Ambitious Executive So-and-So hatches a devilishly clever initiative to hitch her star to. But to secure top management's approval, she needs evidence that her idea has merit. So she charters a task force, allegedly to study the problem for which she already has the solution. The possible rub: If the group is free to make up its own mind, it just may recommend a different solution, which she will have to accept—hmmm—or bury, to widespread dismay. On the other hand, if she railroads her own idea through, bright underlings may at some point divine that they have been had.

•**The ambassador syndrome.** This is a high-tech variant of the dummy task force, identified by Gifford Pinchot III, a consultant and the author of *Intrapreneuring*, a treatise on how to promote entrepreneurship within a large corporation. The brass get hip to the trendy notion that to develop a workable new product quickly, they will have to "tear down the walls between departments." They form a team with representatives from marketing, manufacturing, all the major corporate functions. But instead of giving team members real power to innovate, the departments merely send ambassadors, who must check back with their bosses before committing to anything.

•**Rock-hard controls.** "It's surprisingly tough to simplify control systems," Pinchot finds. Yes, we want innovation, the company says, but you still have to get the usual fourteen approvals for any initiative.

•**The business-of-a-certain-size ploy.** This goes beyond that sure-fire innovation stopper long favored by the brass: "We are a big company; we only want to look at opportunities that will have sales of a couple hundred million

CONTINUES ON PAGE 202

201

THE POLITICS OF INNOVATION
Continued from page 201

within three years." As professor Robert Burgelman of the Stanford business school points out, the more subtle threat may be letting the new business go ahead, but setting financial hurdles that require its management to force it, as a gardener forces flowers. The venture may meet its targets, but when it needs to take the next step—say, to introduce a second product—the whole jerry-built structure collapses.

•**The no-special-treatment reflex.** We're serious this time, say the corporate Olympians to the would-be innovator. We want you to go ahead and act just like an entrepreneur. You mean you want me to work unconscionable hours, alienate others by my unrelenting pursuit of the dream, and perhaps jeopardize my career? Yes. Well, how about paying me extra if we hit big, or giving me a little piece of the action? What, comes back the outraged response, and screw up our artfully crafted compensation system?

•**They're-not-serious cynicism.** After enough of the above, the company's middle managers, the parties most threatened by innovation, adopt what Foster calls "cunningly cynical views about top management's intentions." By the time the brass finally do get serious, the middlings have persuaded everyone else not to take the muck-a-mucks at their word.

How to overcome the politics, to give innovation a chance? First discard the easy, romantic myths. The innovator as creative zealot, for example, championing his idea in the face of dragonlike bureaucracy, fighting his way to glory in the marketplace. "It happens that way maybe one time in thirty," says McKinsey's Foster. Or the perhaps more appealing belief that all we need to achieve innovation is participative management. Liberating everyone to do his job more as he sees fit may be a necessary condition for lasting innovation, but it isn't sufficient in itself. The process still has to be managed.

From the top. No way around it, the brass really have to send loud and clear signals that they are committed to the cause. They may do this by appointing a rising star as the corporate czar of new product development. Or by spending significant time in the labs and with the innovators. Best yet, they can offer even more tangible indications of their backing, like monetary rewards proportionate to the new idea's success.

It helps to hold up a cause that everyone can rally around. Quality, for instance, or a flat-out declaration from the top that three years hence, they expect X percent of the company's revenues and profits to come from new businesses. Then write some concrete measure of progress toward this goal into the performance each manager is appraised on.

Just about every expert on innovation agrees that to get a new business started, you do need one of those multifunctional teams: maybe four people, one each from design, manufacturing, marketing, and finance. Top management should help them find support anywhere they can in the organization. A good sponsor high up may be crucial: He can locate resources, run political interference, and ask questions along the lines of "But have you thought about how that might sit with so-and-so?"

Evaluate the team as a team, and reward them as a team. The experts cite a number of intriguing new ways to com-

CONTINUES ON PAGE 204

101
CREATIVE
PROBLEM
SOLVING
TECHNIQUES

203

THE POLITICS OF INNOVATION
Continued from page 203

pensate innovators: phantom stock in the venture, even special employment contracts to take the folks out of the standard pay hierarchy. Won't others in the company be envious? They might, except for one wrinkle: At the cutting edge of thinking on the subject, the emerging wisdom is that you should require would-be innovators to put something of their own at risk in a startup. Like money, or maybe even their jobs. For instance, you might make them buy in, literally, by paying for that phantom stock.

To be sure, this runs counter to much current thinking on innovation, all the stuff that says that only when employees feel secure about their jobs will they take the risk of proposing new ideas. But Foster and Kuczmarski keep coming back to a single word in describing what it truly takes to get a venture up and running: tough. *It's* tough; *you* have to be tough. At the very least, tough enough to cut through the politics.

CONTROL

No specific techniques are presented here. Several of the approaches described in Chapter 3 are control techniques. Traditional control activities overlap with analyzing the environment and identifying and recognizing the problem. Benchmarking and best practices, for example, are control activities as well as creative ways of scanning the environment. Similarly, Camelot fulfills the conceptual model of control, that is, set standards, measure performance, compare the two, and then take the necessary corrective actions.

SELLING IDEAS AT AMEX

Sarah M. Nolan, executive vice-president of the Insurance and Investment Group at American Express Travel Related Services Co., developed the idea of Membership Savings, a program that allows customers to make contributions to a money-market-type account when paying their American Express card bills. According to Nolan, three elements that can turn ideas into products are homework, advice, and conviction. The basis for the Membership Savings idea was a product called Privileged Assets, which allowed members to save for retirement each month when paying their American Express bill. The success of this product suggested that people of all ages were interested in saving. The "homework" for Membership Savings consisted of two waves of focus-group research that introduced the product and defined the features desired by card members. The next step was to seek advice from senior managers with expertise in marketing to American Express card members. The third stage of the project was the final request for funding.

Source: "Selling Your Ideas to Management," *Working Woman*, (September 1990), pp. 85, 87.

THE INNOVATIVE EDGE IN ACTION 6.2

101
CREATIVE
PROBLEM
SOLVING
TECHNIQUES

205

REFERENCES

[1] Most of this discussion is based on Simon Majaro, *The Creative Gap: Managing Ideas for Profit* (London: Longman, 1988), 44-50. I have taken his basic concept and revised it to make its use consistent with other such matrices, for example, those used in portfolio management.

[2] I have expanded Majaro's concept a bit here. He views screening as a two step process. I have combined both steps into one, and used the matrix to do both. He uses it to do only the first part of screening, that mostly concerned with the organization's needs. I add market factors.

[3] For a discussion see James M. Higgins and Julian W. Vincze, *Strategic Management: Text and Cases*, 5th. ed. (Ft. Worth, Texas; Dryden Press, 1993), pp. 266-268.

[4] Bryan W. Mattimore, "Brainstormers Boot Camp," *Success* (October 1991), p. 28.

[5] Bryan W. Mattimore, ibid.

[6] Simon Majaro, *The Creative Gap: Managing Ideas for Profit* (London: Longman, 1988), p. 153.

[7] This material is taken from Roger von Oech, *A Kick in the Seat of the Pants* (New York: Perennial Library, 1986), pp. 12-19.

[8] Ibid., p. 16.

[9] Don Frey, "Learning the Ropes: My Life as a Product Champion," *Harvard Business Review* (September-October 1991), pp. 46–56.

[10] Kurt Lewin, *Field, Theory, and Social Science: Selected Theoretical Papers* (New York: Harper & Row, 1951).

[11] Author's consultation with managers in this division.

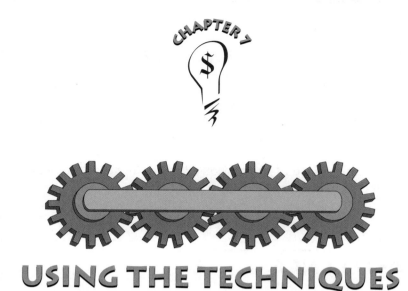

USING THE TECHNIQUES

This book closes with two brief discussions: one on the use of intuition in innovation, the other on using the techniques described in this book.

USING YOUR INTUITION

Intuition can and should be used in all stages of creative problem solving. Rationality is a major contributor to the problem-solving process, but rationality alone does not result in the best solutions to many problems, especially complex problems. If rationality alone sufficed, computers would make all the decisions. As problems become more complex, the need to use intuition in problem solving becomes more critical. Research and experience indicate that complex problems almost defy rational analysis. They require the ability to see connections among numerous variables, connections that often are not discernible in the rational approach.[1] The advice offered by many experts is to trust your intuition, to let it help you solve problems. To gain skill in using intuition in solving problems, it is necessary to practice doing so in real situations as well as decision simulations. The third book in this trilogy, *Escape From the Maze: Improving Personal and Group Creativity*, discusses intuition in greater depth.

101
CREATIVE
PROBLEM
SOLVING
TECHNIQUES

207

USING THE TECHNIQUES

Let me close by emphasizing the importance of consciously planning to use these techniques. These techniques are extremely helpful, but only if you use them. Read them first, then formulate a plan to use them and integrate them into your problem-solving efforts, those of your work group, and if possible, those of the rest of your organization. Be committed to using them.

REFERENCES

[1] Weston Agor, "The Logic of Intuition: How Top Executives Make Important Decisions," *Organizational Dynamics* (Winter 1986), pp. 5-18; Dina Ingber, "Inside the Executive Mind," *Success* (January 1984), pp. 33-37; Daniel Coleman, "Success for Executives Relies on Own Kind of Intelligence," *New York Times* (July 13, 1984), pp. C1, C2; and Henry Mintzberg, "Planning on the Left Side, Managing on the Right," *Harvard Business Review* (July-August 1976), pp. 49-58.

APPENDIX I
A Quick Guide to the Processes

	PROCESS:	BRIEF DESCRIPTION AND/OR BEST USED FOR:
STAGE: ENVIRONMENTAL ANALYSIS		
1	Comparisons against others: benchmarking, best practices, race against phantom competitors	Highly competitive strategic situations for finding quality/cost problems
2	Hire futurists, consultants	When an outside view will help, when you don't have the manpower or funds for internal effort
3	Monitor weak signals	Identifying weak signals in the market, strategic scanning, strategic issue identification
4	Opportunity searches	New situations, new applications of current knowledge, strategic situations
STAGE: PROBLEM RECOGNITION		
1	Camelot	To make sure problems haven't been overlooked, uses an idealized situation
2	Checklists	Finding problem with existing products/services/operations; developing promotional ideas
3	Inverse brainstorming	When routine techniques haven't suggested many problems
4	Limericks and parodies	When straightforward approaches haven't produced many problems or insights, to add humor
5	Listing complaints	Looking for internal or customer problems
6	Responding to someone else	When someone else offers opportunities or problems
7	Role playing	Group, personal insights into simple and complex problems, especially good for interpersonal and customer relations problems
8	Suggestion programs	Systematic problem recognition when employee participation is sought
9	Workouts and other work group/team approaches	Complex problems where group inputs and team building are important. Workouts are best used at a retreat

	STAGE: PROBLEM IDENTIFICATION	
1	Bounce it off someone else	When you want to make sure you haven't overlooked anything
2	Consensus building	When a group definition of the problem is important
3	Draw a picture of the problem	Complex problems use visualization to "see" problem
4	Experience kit	To get people more personally involved in the issue
5	Fishbone diagram	Seeks better understanding of causes
6	"King of the mountain"	Group definition of problem, a fun activity
7	Redefining the problem or opportunity	Increased insight into real problem
8	Rewrite objectives several different ways	For different views of the problem
9	"Squeeze and stretch"	For understanding causes of more complex problems
10	What do you know?	To get started on problems
11	What patterns exist?	For understanding more complex problems
12	Why-why diagram	To better understand the causes of a complex problem
	STAGE: MAKING ASSUMPTIONS	
1	Assumption reversal	For understanding assumptions and gaining possible solutions
	STAGE: ALTERNATIVE GENERATION, INDIVIDUAL BASED	
1	Analogies and metaphors	When a new perspective is needed
2	Analysis of past solutions	Applying other people's solutions to your problem
3	Association	When new zest is needed, generates lots of ideas
4	Attribute association chains	Product/service changes
5	Attribute listing	Product/service changes
6	Back to the customer	For satisfying customer needs; similar to Back to the Sun

7	"Back to the sun"	Focused association
8	Circle of opportunity	Changing product or service, when a new approach is needed
9	Computer programs	Complex problems. Computer programs generally lead you through CPS stages, offer suggestions. Some enhance processes such as brainstorming
10	Deadlines	To put pressure on to increase creativity
11	Direct analogies	To transfer knowledge from one field to another
12	Establish idea sources	Find sources which can offer solutions
13	Examine it with the senses	New insights, complex or simple problems, focused association
14	FCB grid	Positioning products
15	Focused-object	Similar to association and forced relationship techniques
16	Fresh eye	When insiders are having trouble seeing the forest for the trees
17	Idea bits and racking	Organizing your ideas, complex problems
18	Idea notebook	Recording ideas for later reference
19	Input-Output	Engineering, operations management; generates a number of possible solutions
20	Listening to music	Generating alternatives/opportunities through subconscious
21	Mind mapping	Generate new ideas, identify all issues and subissues to a problem, develop intuitive capacity
22	Name possible uses	Generating new uses for a product
23	The Napoleon technique	Gaining totally new insights, when other techinques have failed
24	Organized random search	Simple ways to get new thoughts

25	Personal analogies	To get people more personally involved in the problem
26	Picture stimulation	Uses visualization to improve insight
27	Product improvement checklist (PICL)	Create new products/services, improve old ones
28	Relatedness	Generating lots of ideas fast, similar to association
29	Relational words	Artistic efforts, writing, or product name/development
30	Reversal—dereversal	Problems you don't seem to be making much headway on
31	Rolling in the Grass of Ideas	When lots of ideas, concepts are needed to produce new insights
32	7 X 7 technique	Organizing your ideas, complex problems
33	Sleeping/dreaming on it	Complex or simple problems, generates alternatives/opportunities through subconscious
34	Two words technique	Simple problems where new insights are needed
35	Using the computer to stimulate creativity	Applying many of the above techniques with software
36	Verbal checklist for creativity	Create new products/services, improve existing ones
37	Visualization	When you need to "see" the problem better. Can be used with other processes. Offers new insights
38	What if ...	Strategic planning; complex or simple problems, scenario forecasting

	STAGE: ALTERNATIVE GENERATION, GROUP BASED	
1	Brainstorming	Generating numerous alternatives; simple problems
2	Brainwriting	Alternative to brainstorming
3	Brainwriting pool	Alternative to brainstorming

4	Brainwriting 6-3-5	Alternative to brainstorming
5	Creative imaging	Complex problems, uses visualization
6	Creative leap	Complex problems where major results are needed, includes imaging
7	Creativity circles	Complex or simple problems where group input is desired, expansion of quality circle concept
8	Crawford slip method	Going beyond brainstorming; complex problems
9	Delphi technique	Complex problems to be solved by expert opinion
10	Excursion technique	Problems which other techniques have not solved, great for new perspectives
11	The gallery method	Using visuals to prompt brainstorming
12	The Gordon/Little technique	Good for stepping back from the problem
13	Group decision support systems	Using computer hardware and software to aid group decision process
14	Idea board	Non-urgent problems, similar to gallery method without time constraints
15	Idea triggers	Getting people involved in the issue
16	Innovation committee	Complex or simple problems, like creativity circles
17	Intercompany innovation groups	Where other outside firms can help, popular in Europe and gaining popularity in U.S.
18	Lions den	Two teams, one presents problems to the other to generate solutions
19	The lotus blossom technique	Complex or simple problems, especially good for developing strategic scenarios
20	The Mitsubishi brainstorming method	Brainstorming w/mapping for complex problems
21	Morphological analysis	Changing product or service

22	The NHK method	Complex problems
23	Nominal group technique	Eliminating affect of dominant personality in group
24	Phillips 66	To encourage participation brainstorming by breaking larger groups into groups of six
25	Photo-excursion	Visual stimulation of brainstorming
26	Pin card technique	Alternative to brainstorming
27	Scenario writing	Complex problems, especially strategic planning
28	The SIL method	Alternative to brainstorming for complex problems
29	Storyboarding	Complex problems, identifying issues, generating numerous alternatives
30	Synectics	Complex problems, brainstorming with analogies, metaphors, excursion. Heavy on critical analysis
31	Take five	Going beyond brainstorming; complex problems
32	The TKJ method	Complex problems, uses cards, diagrams and association
	STAGE: CHOICE	
1	Screening matrix for ideas	Choosing solutions to all types of problems
2	Dot voting	Choosing solutions to all types of problems
	STAGE: IMPLEMENTATION	
1	How-how diagram	Determining necessary actions for successful implementation
2	Be a warrior	Getting ideas adopted in company
3	Force field analysis	Analyzing roadblocks to implementation
	STAGE: CONTROL	
	See Environmental Analysis, Problem Recognition and Problem Identification	

INDEX

101
CREATIVE
PROBLEM
SOLVING
TECHNIQUES

215

101
CREATIVE
PROBLEM
SOLVING
TECHNIQUES

217

101
CREATIVE
PROBLEM
SOLVING
TECHNIQUES

219

101
CREATIVE
PROBLEM
SOLVING
TECHNIQUES

221

ABOUT THE AUTHOR:

James M. Higgins, PhD, is an author, consultant, professor, and entrepreneur. He is the author of 6 college texts on strategy, management, and human relations. He has recently completed, *101 Creative Problem Solving Techniques: The Handbook of New Ideas for Business,* which is used in his seminars. His next two books, *Innovate or Evaporate: Test and Improve Your Organization's IQ—Its Innovation Quotient* and *Escape From the Maze: Increasing Personal and Group Creativity,* will be published in 1995. He is the author of numerous articles and cases.

He is an experienced consultant, working with people and firms since 1985, to increase levels of innovation as well as to solve particular problems. Dr. Higgins also consults with organizations on strategic planning and in behavioral areas such as motivation, leadership, communication, and stress management. His clients have included firms such as several divisions of Walt Disney Companies, Sun Trust Bank, Skopbank (Helsinki), and Florida Info-Management Services. He has been a consultant since 1973.

Dr. Higgins is Professor of Management at the Roy E. Crummer Graduate School of Business at Rollins College in Winter Park, Florida.

101 Creative Problem Solving Techniques provides his insights into vital creative processes. He believes that "Until your competitors learn these processes, knowing them will help you achieve a sizeable competitive advantage, so learn them before they do."

101
CREATIVE
PROBLEM
SOLVING
TECHNIQUES

223